μMPS3
Principles of Operation

The Virtual Square Lab

Michael Goldweber

Xavier University

Renzo Davoli

Università di Bologna

μMPS3, μMPS2, μMPS, MPS, μARM, Pandos, Kaya are products of the Virtual Square Lab.
See `virtualsquare.org/`
The μMPS3 home page is `virtualsquare.org/umps`

ISBN: 978-1-716-47640-2

Contents

List of Figures

List of Tables

Preface

In my junior year as an undergraduate I took a course titled "Systems Programming." The goal of this course was for each student to write a small, simple multitasking operating system, in S/360 assembler, for an IBM S/360. The students were given use of a machine emulator, Assist-V, for the development process. Assist, was a S/360 assembler programming environment. (Think SPIM for the 70's.) Assist-V was an extension of Assist that supported privileged instructions in addition to various emulated "attached" devices. The highlight of the course was if your operating system ran correctly (or at least without discernible errors), you would be granted the opportunity, in the dead of night, to boot the University's mainframe, an IBM S/370, with your operating system. (Caveat: The University used VM, IBM's virtual machine technology. Hence students didn't actually boot the whole machine with their OS's, but just one VM partition. Nevertheless, booting/running a VM partition and booting/running the whole machine are isomorphic tasks.) No question, booting and running a handful of tasks concurrently on the University's mainframe with my own OS was one of the highlights of my undergraduate education!

For my senior project I undertook to update Assist-V to the S/370 ISA. Since neither Assist nor Assist-V supported floating point instructions, this basically meant adding virtual memory support to Assist-V. I recall my surprise in the mid-1980's receiving an email from some institution that was still using Assist-V/370 to support their operating systems course.

My experience of writing a complete operating system repeated itself in graduate school. In this case the machine emulator was the Cornell Hypothetical Instruction Processor (CHIP); a made up architecture that was a cross between a PDP-11 and an IBM S/370. The operating system design was a three phase/layer affair called HOCA by its creator. While there was no real machine to test with, the thrill and sense of accomplishment of successfully completing the task, to say nothing of the many lessons learned throughout the experience were no less than the earlier experience.

Time passed and like Assist-V/370, CHIP fell out of use. (It only ran on Dec Vaxen or Sun 3's. It also defied at least two serious attempts at being ported to more current platforms.) A professor myself, now teaching operating systems, I experimented with the courseware systems of the day. Sadly these tools, while of very high quality, all fell short of the pedagogic experience of having students write a complete operating system supporting virtual memory, a host of device types, and being able to run a set of tasks concurrently.

In the late 1990's Professor Renzo Davoli and one of his graduate students, Mauro Morsiani, in the spirit of both Assist-V/370 and CHIP, created MPS, a MIPS 3000 machine emulator that not only authentically emulated the processor (still no floating point), but also faithfully emulated five different device categories. Furthermore, they updated the HOCA project for this new architecture. Once again, students could take their operating system, developed and debugged on MPS (which also contained an excellent debugging facility) and run it unchanged on a real machine.

Unfortunately, modern architectures like the MIPS 3000 which are designed to achieve super high speed operation can be overly complex in their detail, obscuring the basic underlying features and unnecessarily complicating students' understanding. Hence we (Professor Davoli and myself) learned via class testing that MPS due to the complexity of MIPS' virtual memory management was unsuitable for undergraduates. In the MIPS architecture, virtual memory is always on, all address translation is performed through a small fixed size TLB, and hence even the OS maintained page tables for itself and user processes are kept in virtual memory. Furthermore, the physical address space for the kernel and its data structures are permanently disjoint from its virtual address space. While these RISC-design features allow for an extremely fast processor they complicate introductory students' understanding; in particular with the circularity of an OS always running with VM on and whose page tables are kept in virtual memory.

In 2004, Renzo and I set out to create μMPS – a pedagogically appropriate machine emulator suitable for use by undergraduates. The primary design goal of μMPS was to implement a virtual memory management subsystem that more closely matched the conceptual description found in popular introductory OS texts.

μMPS3, in a very real sense, represents our third, though depending on how one counts, one might say, fourth iteration of designing an architecture based on a real-world architecture, and creating an emulator for that architecture that supports both peripheral devices, and an excellent debugging environment. Interested readers are invited to read the *Principles of Operation* for

- μMPS - Our first attempt at solving this problem. This version introduced a VM-bit, BIOS code to handle TLB-Refill events, a CISC-style exception vector, and a paged-segmentation virtual memory architecture.

- μMPS2 - Multiprocessor support was added along with a major upgrade of the GUI and debugging facilities.

- μARM - The systems educational community started to experiment with architectures more familiar to students, e.g. ARM. As part of this movement, we created μARM, the ARM-inspired version of μMPS based on the ARM7TDMI variant.

Lessons learned over the 16 year span between μMPS and μMPS3 (in brief):

- The MIPS architecture, though less familiar by name to students, is still the cleanest and easiest to understand for undergraduate students. Pedagogy should always triumph over familiarity.

- Hard and fast rules, with respect to address translation, work best. We substituted the VM-bit for a machine configurable TLB Floor Address; a fixed address below which address translation is disabled.

- Less is more. Having the BIOS routines handle TLB-Refill events ultimately obscured student understanding.

- Don't mix architectural philosophies. The CISC-style exception vector did not match what students were seeing in their OS texts. The same was true for segmentation. μMPS3 implements paging without segmentation.

- Students understanding of tape devices is equivalent to their experience with 8-track players. Support for tape devices was replaced with support for flash memory devices.

- Students prefer to work on their own machines, rather than off of a departmental server. While all night coding sessions remain "standard practice," these now occur in student dormitories, apartments, and bedrooms, rather than in a university lab. Hence, installation procedures and software dependencies need to be manageable to an undergraduate student. μMPS3 now uses the standard gnu gcc MIPS cross compiler and is itself compiled and installed using CMake.

Renzo and I wish to offer our heartfelt thanks and gratitude to:

- Mauro Morsiani. Mauro generously donated his time to modify MPS into μMPS. μMPS and the accompanying Kaya Project Guide were originally released in 2004.

- Tomislav Jonjic, who updated the GUI and added multiprocessor support, creating μMPS2. μMPS2 is 100% backward compatible with μMPS.

- Marco Melletti, who in 2017, created μARM.

- Mattia Biondi, who graciously and competently undertook the development work in updating μMPS2 to μMPS3.

μMPS3 is NOT backwards compatible with μMPS2 (nor μMPS). We believe that our third time is a charm and that the architecture is simple, but not too simple and that all the relevant issues related to machine organization and operating systems are clearly visible and not clouded by unnecessary detail.

μMPS3 is designed to host any number of architecture and operating systems related projects. One in particular is Pandos, which like μMPS3 was created and is supported by the Virtual Square Lab.

As the date below indicates, the μMPS3 project took place during the 2020 Covid-19 pandemic. While I and my wife planned on residing in Bologna, Italy for six months, we returned home to Cincinnati, OH after two and a half months, in March of 2020. Though our time in Bologna was cut short, I wish to thank the University of Bologna in general and Renzo Davoli, my long-time friend and partner in "CS" crime in particular for their hospitality and support.

Finally we wish to thank our wives, Alessandra and Mindy without whose inexhaustible patience projects such as this would never see the light of day.

Michael Goldweber
May, 2020

Part I
The Architecture of μMPS3

Computer system architecture is the attributes of a computing system as seen by the programmer, i.e. the conceptual structure and functional behavior, as distinct from the organization of the data flows and controls, the logic design, and the physical implementation.

Brooks & Amdahl, Blaauw & Brooks - on the Architecture of the IBM System/360

1

Introduction to μMPS3

μMPS3 is not a real chip, nor a real machine, though there is no reason why it could not be. μMPS3 is an architecture/system specification designed to aid students in their study of operating systems. As such, it is based on the MIPS R2/3000 RISC architecture.

umps3 is a software artifact, that faithfully emulates a μMPS3 machine. umps3 faithfully executes μMPS3/MIPS assembly created by the standard gnu gcc MIPS cross compiler.[1]

Part I of this manual describes the μMPS3 system as it might come delivered from a manufacturer: complete with a description of supported peripheral devices, included BIOS routines and a software library. As such, it blurs the line between the umps3 emulator (e.g. the μMPS3 Machine Configuration Panel), and a hypothetical μMPS3 machine.

Part II of this manual focuses on toolchain development (which theoretically could have been included in Part I) and the use of the umps3 emulator.

---

[1]Unlike previous versions, μMPS3 does not rely on a special development toolchain.

1

1.1 μMPS3 and The MIPS R2/3000

μMPS3 takes the MIPS R2/3000 architecture as its starting point and introduces a number of changes/simplifications. Interested readers are referred to the official MIPS processor handbook to fully understand our starting point.

In particular, μMPS3 differs from a MIPS R2/3000 device in the following ways:

- No support for floating point operations.

- No pipelining; all instructions execute in a single clock cycle.

- A simplified, though comprehensive device interface. μMPS3 supports up to eight instances of five different classes of emulated peripheral devices: disks, printers, terminals, network cards, and flash storage devices. [Chapter 5]

- A sophisticated, integrated debugging environment. [Chapter 12]

- A simplified address space. As with a MIPS R2/3000, μMPS3 divides the conceptual address space into four chunks: three kernel address spaces (two .5 GB and one 1 GB, **kseg0**, **kseg1**, and **kseg2** respectively) and one 2 GB user space - **kuseg**. However, their address ordering has been reversed. [Chapter 6]

- User configurable TLB size and RAM size. The number of slots in the TLB (associative cache used in virtual address translation) as well as the number of 4 KB frames of RAM are user configurable via the μMPS3 Machine Configuration Panel. [Section 12.2.1]

- User configurable TLB Floor Address. [Section 6.3.1] Unlike the MIPS R2/3000 where address translation is always enabled for all address, μMPS3 implements a user configurable parameter, TLB Floor Address. All addresses below TLB Floor Address are understood as physical addresses, while all addresses greater than or equal to TLB Floor Address are subject to a logical to physical address translation. There are four possible settings for TLB Floor Address:

  - VM Off.
  - 0x8000.0000: VM is off for all three kernel address spaces and on for **kuseg**.

- 0x4000.0000: VM is off for **kseg0** and **kseg1**, and on for **kseg2** and **kuseg**.

- RAMTOP: VM is off for **kseg0** and part of **kseg1**. VM is on for **kuseg**, **kseg2**, and the (upper) portion of **kseg1** above RAMTOP. If the logical address also exists as a physical address, then that address is used, otherwise, an MMU address translation is performed.

- User programmable/replaceable BIOS/firmware code. The behavior of the default BIOS code provided with μMPS3 is described in this guide. However, given the pedagogical purpose of μMPS3, students have the opportunity to examine, alter or even rewrite the BIOS routines, which are provided via MIPS assembly files. [Chapter 8]

All other aspects of μMPS3 behavior mimics a real R2/3000 MIPS processor. This includes, branch-delay slots (invisible to programmers working in C), exception handling, **CP0** co-processors including MMU processing, and multi-processor support/control.

This manual, along with a MIPS processor handbook to document the integer instruction set of μMPS3, presents a complete description of the μMPS3 virtual machine. Since development for the μMPS3 is typically done in C using a cross compiler to generate μMPS3 code, it is unlikely that one will make much (any?) use of the MIPS processor handbook.

There are times at which the student programmer, writing in C, needs to directly access specific machine registers, or assembly instructions. The μMPS3 installation includes a library (`libumps`) to facilitate these assembly-level operations from a C program. [Chapter 7]

1.2 Notational conventions

- Words being defined are *italicized.*

- Register, fields and instructions are **bold**-marked.

- Field **F** of register **R** is denoted **R.F**.

- Bits of storage are numbered right-to-left, starting with 0.

- The i-th bit of a storage unit named **N** is denoted **N**[i].

- Memory addresses and operation codes are given in hexadecimal and presented in big-endian format.

- All diagrams illustrate memory and going from low addresses to high addresses using a left to right, bottom to top orientation.

- Cross references to other Sections or Chapters where one can find more detailed information are enclosed in square brackets: [Section 1.2]

2

System Structure and Overview

2.1 Components of μMPS3

μMPS3 contains

- A processor. μMPS3 provides support for up to 16 processors. By default, at system start/restart only Processor 0 is active. [Chapter 9]

- A system control coprocessor, **CP0**, incorporated into each processor.

- A memory device. A volatile random-access memory device, divided into 4 KB frames, whose size is user configurable from 32 KB up to 2 MB in size - 512 frames of RAM. While the (artificial) limit of 2 MB may seem small, it is more than adequate for the kind of projects μMPS3 was created to support.

  Memory is "installed" starting from address 0x2000.0000. The first 0.5 GB of the physical address space, called **kseg0** (0x0000.0000 - 0x2000.0000), is always present and is, for the most part, "Read Only." [Section 6.1]

- BIOS routines (e.g. firmware). In addition to bootstrap code, a routine automatically executed at system start/restart, μMPS3 automatically invokes

5

various BIOS routines as part of its exception handling protocol. [Chapters 3 and 8]

All of the BIOS routines (e.g. bootstrap and exception handlers) are user programmable. A default BIOS is provided, but can be modified or replaced.

- Peripheral devices: up to eight instances for each of five device classes: disks, flash storage devices, printers, terminals, and network interface devices. [Chapter 5]

- A system bus connecting all the system components.

- The `libumps` library to facilitate C-language access to the **CP0** registers and certain MIPS assembly instructions. `libumps` also "extends" the MIPS ISA with seven new instructions particularly useful for writing operating systems. The `libumps` library is fully described in Chapter 7.

Each of μMPS3's processors implements an accurate emulation of a MIPS R2/3000 RISC processor, providing

- A RISC-type integer instruction set based on the load/store paradigm.

- A 32-bit *word* length for both instructions and registers. All physical addresses are 32 bits wide. The address space therefore is 2^{32} = 4 GB; every single 8-bit byte has its own address. *doublewords* are 64 bits and *halfwords* are 16 bits.

- 32 general purpose registers (**GPR**) denoted **$0**...**$31**

  – Register **$0** is hardwired to zero (0). This register ignores writes and always returns zero on read.

  – Registers **$1**...**$31** support both loads and stores. In addition to a numeric designation, each register is also referenced via its standard MIPS mnemonic designation. Ten of these registers are for general computations while the rest are reserved for various purposes. The most important reserved register is stack pointer **$28**, denoted **SP**. Registers **$26** and **$27**, denoted **k0** and **k1** respectively are reserved solely for kernel use.

- Two special registers, **HI** and **LO**, are for holding the results from multiplication and division operations.

- A program counter, **PC**, for instruction addressing.

- A system control coprocessor, **CP0**, which provides:

  - Support for two processor operation modes: kernel-mode and user-mode. [Section 2.3]

  - Support for exception handling. [Chapter 3]

  - A processor Local Timer capable of generating interrupts. [Section 4.1.4]

  - A Memory Management Unit (MMU) for the translation of addresses above the TLB Floor Address. [Section 6.3]

CP0 implements ten control registers.

  - Five support MMU operations: **Index**, **Random**, **EntryHi**, **EntryLo**, and **BadVAddr**. [Section 6.4]

  - Two support exception handling: **Cause** [section 3.3] and **EPC**.

  - **PRID** – a read-only *processor ID* register (an integer $i \in [0..15]$)

  - **Timer** – the processor Local Timer. [Section 4.1.4]

  - **Status** – the processor status register. [Section 2.3]

2.1.1 The μMPS3 Address Space

The 4 GB address space is divided into four chunks as follows [Section 6.2]:

- **kseg0** (0x0000.0000 - 0x2000.0000): This mostly "read only" 0.5 GB section is the "installed EPROM" BIOS memory region. **kseg0** holds the BIOS routines, device registers, bus device registers, and multiprocessor communication/support structures.

- **kseg1** (0x2000.0000 - 0x4000.0000): This 0.5 GB section is designed to hold the kernel/OS.

- **kseg2** (0x4000.0000 - 0x8000.0000): This 1 GB section is for use when implementing a sophisticated operating system.

- **kuseg** (0x8000.0000- 0xFFFF.FFFF): This 2 GB section is for user programs.

Access to to **kseg0**, **kseg1**, and **kseg2** require the processor to be in kernel-mode. Access to **kuseg** is possible from both the kernel-mode and user-mode processor setting.

2.2   Processor State

A *processor state* is defined as the set of values that must be saved when an executing process is interrupted so that it can be restarted at a later point in time as if it had not been interrupted. Essentially, a processor state is the contents of all the user and control registers: the current *state* of the processor. Reloading a processor state allows a process to continue executing from where it left off.

A processor state in μMPS3 is defined as a 35 word block that contains the following registers:

- The **EntryHi CP0** register. This register contains the current **ASID**, which is essentially the process ID (**EntryHi.ASID**). [Section 6.3.2]

- The **Cause CP0** register. [Section 3.3]

- The **Status CP0** register. [Section 2.3]

- The **PC**.

- 29 words for the **GPR** registers. **GPR** registers $0, $k0, and $k1 are excluded.

- The **HI** and **LO** registers.

Appendix A illustrates a C language struct definition of a processor state (state_t).

2.3   The Status Register

Status is a read/writable **CP0** register that controls the usability of the coprocessors, the processor mode of operation (kernel vs. user), and the interrupt masking bits.

All bit fields in the **Status** register are read/writable. In particular:

31		28	27	26	25	24	23	22	21		16	15			8	7	6	5	4	3	2	1	0
	CU		TE					BEV					Interrupt Mask (IM)					KUo	IEo	KUp	IEp	KUc	IEc

Figure 2.1: Status Register

- **IEc**: bit 0 - The "current" global interrupt enable bit. When 0, regardless of the settings in **Status.IM** all interrupts are disabled. When 1, interrupt acceptance is controlled by **Status.IM**.

- **KUc**: bit 1 - The "current" kernel-mode user-mode control bit. When **Status.KUc**=0 the processor is in kernel-mode.

- **IEp & KUp**: bits 2-3 - the "previous" settings of the **Status.IEc** and **Status.KUc**.

- **IEo & KUo**: bits 4-5 - the "previous" settings of the **Status.IEp** and **Status.KUp** - denoted the "old" bit settings.

  These six bits; **IEc, KUc, IEp, KUp, IEo,** and **KUo** act as 3-slot deep **KU/IE** bit stacks. Whenever an exception is raised the stack is pushed [Section 3.1] and whenever an interrupted execution stream is restarted, the stack is popped. [Section 7.4]

- **IM**: bits 8-15 - The Interrupt Mask. An 8-bit mask that enables/disables external interrupts. When a device raises an interrupt on the i-th line, the processor accepts the interrupt only if the corresponding **Status.IM[i]** bit is on.

- **BEV**: bit 22 - The Bootstrap Exception Vector. This bit determines which BIOS routines get called by the hardware when an exception is raised. When **Status.BEV**=1, the bootstrap BIOS exception handlers are called. When **Status.BEV**=0, the normal runtime BIOS exception handlers are called. [Section 8.2.1]

- **TE**: Bit 27 - the processor Local Timer enable bit. A 1-bit mask that enables/disables the processor's Local Timer. [Section 4.1.4]

- **CU**: Bits 28-31 - a 4-bit field that controls coprocessor usability. The bits are numbered 0 to 3; Setting **Status.CU[i]** to 1 allows the use of the i-th co-processor. Since μMPS3 only implements **CP0** only **Status.CU[0]** is writable; the other three bits are read-only and permanently set to 0.

Trying to make use of a coprocessor (via an appropriate instruction) without the corresponding coprocessor control bit set to 1 will raise a Coprocessor Unusable exception. In particular untrusted processes can be prevented from **CP0** access by setting **Status.CU[0]**=0. **CP0** is always accessible/usable when in kernel mode (**Status.KUc**=0), regardless of the value of **Status.CU[0]**.

There cannot be greater rudeness than to interrupt another in the current of his discourse.

John Locke

3

Exception Handling

An *exception* is defined as an event that interrupts the current execution stream. There are two broad categories of exceptions:

- TLB-Refill events, a relatively frequent occurrence which is triggered during address translation when no matching entries are found in the TLB. [Section 6.3.3]

- All other exception types, including device interrupts, which, by definition, occur infrequently.

For ease of exposition, the first category will be referred to as TLB-Refill events, while the second category will simply be referred to as exceptions. So, even though a TLB-Refill event is technically an "exception," our use of the term *exception* will refer to all exception types exclusive of TLB-Refill events.

Exceptions can be further broken down as follows:

- *I/O Interrupts (Int)*: A peripheral I/O device or System Timer [Section 4.1] signals that it has completed a previously started operation by causing an interrupt exception. These asynchronous interruptions to the current execution stream are only rarely associated with the current executing process.

   μMPS3 allows for 8 *interrupt lines* to be monitored, with each line supporting a number of devices connected to it. Interrupt lines are numbered 0–7. A

11

lower interrupt line indicates a higher servicing precedence for the devices connected to that line. Only 5 interrupt lines are available for peripheral devices.

- Interrupt line 0 is reserved for inter-processor interrupts. [Section 9.4]
- Line 1 is reserved for the processor Local Timer interrupts. [Section 4.1.4]
- Line 2 is reserved for system-wide Interval Timer interrupts. [Section 4.2]
- Interrupt lines 3–7 are for monitoring interrupts from peripheral devices. [Chapter 5]

- *System Calls (Sys)*: A system call exception occurs whenever the non-privileged **SYSCALL** MIPS assembly instruction is executed. The **SYSCALL** instruction is used by processes to request operating system services.

- *Breakpoint Calls (Bp)*: A breakpoint call exception occurs whenever the non-privileged **BREAK** MIPS assembly instruction is executed. The **BREAK** instruction is used by processes to request operating system services.

  The **SYSCALL** and **BREAK** instructions essentially perform the same function. By convention, **SYSCALL** is used to request operating system services, while **BREAK** is used to support debugging.

- *Page Faults*: In paged, virtual memory systems such as μMPS3, a page fault exception occurs whenever the executing process attempts to access a page not currently resident in RAM, known in the MIPS/μMPS3 world as a TLB-Invalid exception (*TLBL* for loads & *TLBS* for stores). Specifically, for μMPS3 a page fault exception is raised whenever the TLB entry for the referenced page is marked *invalid*. [Chapter 6]

  Each TLB entry also contain a read/write permission bit. A TLB-Modification exception (*Mod*) is raised whenever the executing process attempts to write to a read-only page. In addition to protecting against inadvertent writes, this exception also aids in the implementation of sophisticated page replacement algorithms.

- *Program Traps*: Typically these are associated with errors that the executing process commits. These "self-inflicted" errors include the Address Error, Bus Error, Reserved Instruction, Coprocessor Unusable, and Arithmetic Overflow exceptions.

– Address Error (*AdEL* & *AdES*): This exception is raised whenever

* A load/store/instruction fetch of a word is not aligned on a word boundary.
* A load/store of a halfword is not aligned on a halfword boundary.
* A user-mode access is made to an address below 0x8000.0000 (**kseg0**, **kseg1**, or **kseg2**).

– Bus Error (*IBE* & *DBE*): This exception is raised whenever an access is attempted on a non-existent physical memory location (i.e. an address above RAMTOP) or during a kernel-mode access to any of the undefined or inaccessible portions of the BIOS region. [Section 6.1]

– Reserved Instruction (*RI*): This exception is raised whenever an instruction is ill-formed, not recognizable, or is privileged and is executed in user-mode (**Status.KUc=1**).

– Coprocessor Unusable (*CpU*): This exception is raised whenever an instruction requiring the use of or access to an uninstalled or currently unavailable coprocessor is executed. Since all μMPS3 control registers are implemented as part of **CP0**, access to these registers when **Status.KUc=1** and **Status.CU[0]=0** will raise this exception. **CP0** is always available when in kernel-mode (**Status.KUc=0**).

– Arithmetic Overflow (*OV*): This exception whenever an **ADD** or **SUB** instruction execution results in a 2's-compliment overflow.

3.1 Processor Actions on Exception and TLB-Refill Events

Three of the primary design principles for RISC architectures such as the MIPS R2/3000 and μMPS3 are:

• Keep it simple.

• Make common/frequently occurring operations fast.

• Generalize design and avoid special cases.

While there are both TLB-Refill events and exceptions, the processor performs the same actions for both - designed around the more common TLB-Refill event.

Specifically, the μMPS3 processor will **always** perform the following actions atomically for both exceptions and TLB-Refill events:

1. Load the *Exception PC* (**EPC**) **CP0** register with the current **PC** value.

2. Set the exception cause code in **Cause.ExcCode**. [Section 3.3]

3. Shift/Push the **KU/IE** stacks in the **Status CP0** register in the following manner:

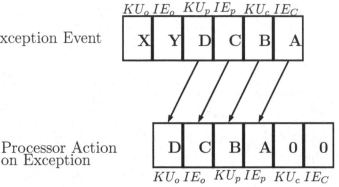

Before Exception Event

Processor Action
on Exception

Figure 3.1: **KU/IE** Stack Push

The "previous" bits of the **Status.KU** and **Status.IE** bits are "pushed" down to the "old" slots, respectively and the "current" bits are "pushed" down to the "previous" slots. Finally, the **Status.KUc** and **Status.IMc** bits are set to zero: kernel-mode with all interrupts masked.

4. Load the **PC** with a new value. This value is

   - 0x0000.0000 for TLB-Refill events. (i.e. The BIOS-TLB-Refill handler)
   - 0x0000.0080 for exceptions. (i.e. The BIOS-Excpt handler)

   These addresses are fixed and immutable and are where the BIOS handlers are loaded. [Chapter 8]

Important Point: The processor always enters the BIOS-TLB-Refill handler and BIOS-Excpt handler in kernel-mode with all interrupts disabled.

Important Point: Returning to a previously interrupted execution stream is accomplished via the **LDST** command which performs the complementary pop operation on the **KU/IE** stacks. Thus returning the processor to whatever interrupt state and mode was in effect when the exception occurred. [Section 7.4]

3.1.1   Additional Processor Actions on Exceptions

Additionally, the μMPS3 processor will also perform the following operations:

- Address Error and Bus Error exceptions: Load the **BadVAddr CP0** register with the offending address.

- Coprocessor Unusable exceptions: Place the appropriate coprocessor number in the **Cause.CE** field.

- Interrupt exceptions: Update the **Cause.IP** field bits to show which lines interrupts are pending.

- MMU-based exceptions (TLB-Refill events, TLB-Modification, and TLB-Invalid exceptions): Load the **BadVAddr CP0** register with the virtual address value that failed translation and load **EntryHi.VPN** with the virtual page number from the virtual address that failed translation.

In summary, when an exception is raised, the processor performs a small number of steps atomically. These include a push operation on the **KU/IE Status** register stacks, saving off the current **PC**, setting the exception code in the **Cause** register, possibly setting some other **CP0** registers (e.g. **BadVAddr**), and finally loading the **PC** with one of two addresses depending on whether the exception was a TLB-Refill event or not. What happens next is up to the BIOS handler whose address is placed in the **PC**.

3.2   BIOS Actions on Exception and TLB-Refill Events

Since the BIOS code sits between the hardware and the kernel, understanding its integration with both the hardware and the kernel is important. However, given the instructional focus of μMPS3, the default/supplied BIOS exception handlers do very little.

As described above, the hardware performs some key tasks. (e.g. Update **Cause.ExcCode**, save the **PC**, turn off interrupts, and enter kernel-mode.) After that the **PC** is loaded with one of two hard-wired BIOS-based addresses:

- 0x0000.0000 for TLB-Refill events. (i.e. The BIOS-TLB-Refill handler)

- 0x0000.0080 for exceptions. (i.e. The BIOS-Excpt handler)

For both TLB-Refill events and exceptions, the default/supplied BIOS handlers perform two tasks and then passes processing along to the kernel.

The source code for the default/supplied BIOS-Excpt handler and BIOS-TLB-Refill handler can be found in exec.S. [Chapter 8]

3.2.1   BIOS Actions on TLB-Refill Events

The default/supplied BIOS code for TLB-Refill events, the BIOS-TLB-Refill handler (i.e. the code found at address 0x0000.0000 will:

- Save off the complete processor state at the time of the TLB-Refill event in a BIOS data structure on the BIOS Data Page. For Processor 0, the address of this processor state is 0x0FFF.F000.

- Set the **PC** and **SP** registers; i.e. pass control to the kernel TLB-Refill event handler. The new values for the **PC** and **SP** registers are found in the BIOS Data Page in the Pass Up Vector. For Processor 0, the address of the Pass Up Vector is 0x0FFF.F900. [Section 8.5]

Important Point: One of the first tasks the operating system code needs to perform at startup is the loading of the Pass Up Vector with the address of the appropriate kernel handler for TLB-Refill events and the value of the **SP** for the kernel.

Important Point: The BIOS-TLB-Refill handler is always entered in kernel-mode with interrupts disabled - see above. Since the BIOS-TLB-Refill handler does not modify the **Status** register, control is therefore passed to the kernel with interrupts disabled and in kernel-mode.

3.2.2   BIOS Actions on Exceptions

The default/supplied BIOS code for exceptions, the BIOS-Excpt handler (i.e. the code found at address 0x0000.0080) will:

- Save off the complete processor state at the time of the exception in a BIOS data structure on the BIOS Data Page. For Processor 0, the address of this processor state is 0x0FFF.F000.

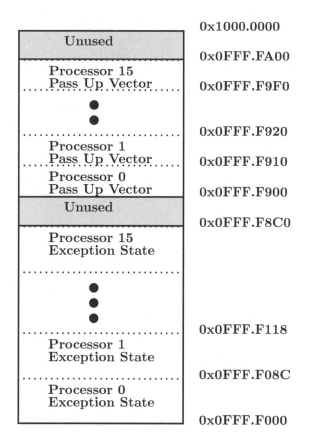

Figure 3.2: Layout of the BIOS Data Page

- Set the **PC** and **SP** registers; i.e. pass control to the kernel exception handler. The new values for the **PC** and **SP** registers are found in the BIOS Data Page in the Pass Up Vector. For Processor 0, the address of the Pass Up Vector is 0x0FFF.F900. [Section 8.5]

Important Point: One of the first tasks the operating system code needs to perform at startup is the loading of the Pass Up Vector with the address of the appropriate kernel handler for exceptions and the value of the **SP** for the kernel.

Important Point: The BIOS-Excpt handler is always entered in kernel-mode with interrupts disabled - see above. Since the BIOS-Excpt handler does not modify the **Status** register, control is therefore passed to the kernel with interrupts disabled and in kernel-mode.

Appendix A.3 details a C-language struct for a Pass Up Vector.

- J-Vectors in init - c

Field #	Address	Field Name
3	(base) + 0xc	**SP** for the kernel event handler
2	(base) + 0x8	kernel exception handler address
1	(base) + 0x4	**SP** for the kernel TLB-Refill event handler
0	(base) + 0x0	kernel TLB-Refill event handler address

Table 3.1: Pass Up Vector Layout

3.3   The Cause Register

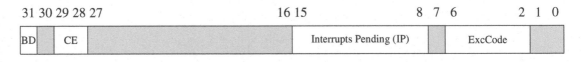

Figure 3.3: **Cause CP0** Register

Cause is a **CP0** register containing information about the current exception and/or pending device interrupts. As described above it is set by the hardware at the time an exception is raised.

The **Cause** fields are all read-only and are defined as follows:

- **ExcCode** (bits 2-6): a 5-bit field that provides a code as to which exception was raised. [Table 3.3]

- **IP** (bits 8-15): an 8-bit field indicating on which interrupt lines interrupts are currently pending. If an interrupt is pending on interrupt line i, then **Cause.IP**[i] is set to 1.

  Important Point: Many interrupt lines may be active at the same time. Furthermore, many devices on the same interrupt line may be requesting service. **Cause.IP** is always up to date, immediately responding to external (peripheral device) and internal (e.g. system timers) device events.

- **CE** (bits 28-29): A 2 bit field which indicates which coprocessor was illegally accessed when a Coprocessor Unusable exception is raised.

- **BD** (bit 31): This bit indicates the last exception raised occurred in a *Branch Delay slot*. Delayed loads and branch delay slots are conventions/techniques

used by fast RISC processors to prevent pipeline slowdowns or stalls.[1] Wh
there are no pipeline stages nor overlapped instruction execution in μMPS3,
delayed loads and branch delay slots are correctly handled. Hence, the **BD**
bit can safely be ignored.

The 13 codes used in **Cause.ExcCode** are:

Number	Code	Description
0	*Int*	External Device Interrupt
1	*Mod*	TLB-Modification Exception
2	*TLBL*	TLB Invalid Exception: on a Load instr. or instruction fetch
3	*TLBS*	TLB Invalid Exception: on a Store instr.
4	*AdEL*	Address Error Exception: on a Load or instruction fetch
5	*AdES*	Address Error Exception: on a Store instr.
6	*IBE*	Bus Error Exception: on an instruction fetch
7	*DBE*	Bus Error Exception: on a Load/Store data access
8	*Sys*	Syscall Exception
9	*Bp*	Breakpoint Exception
10	*RI*	Reserved Instruction Exception
11	*CpU*	Coprocessor Unusable Exception
12	*OV*	Arithmetic Overflow Exception

Table 3.2: Cause Register Status Codes

---

[1] See "MIPS RISC Architecture" by Gary Kane and Joe Heinrich, Prentice Hall, 1992 for more
information.

Any sufficiently advanced technology is indistinguishable from magic.

Arthur C. Clarke

4

Bus Device & Registers

In addition to the peripheral devices discussed in Chapter 5 μMPS3 also implements a *Bus Device*.

The Bus Device acts as the interface between the processor(s), memory, and all supported devices; both internal and peripheral. In particular this device performs the following tasks:

- Clocking services. This includes the two Bus Device clocks: the Time of Day (TOD) clock and Interval Timer, as well as each processor's Local Timer. [Section 4.1]

- Arbitration among the interrupt lines, the devices attached to each interrupt line and the device registers. [Chapter 5]

- Repository of basic system information. As with peripheral devices, the **kseg0** memory area contains special registers associated with the Bus Device called the *Bus Register Area* [Section 4.2]

4.1   System Clocks

μMPS3, via the Bus Device, provides two system-wide clocks, the Time of Day Clock and Interval Timer, plus one local clock per processor.

4.1.1 Time Scale

The clock speed, or Time Scale, is a user configurable value set via the μMPS3 machine configuration panel. [Chapter 12]

The Time Scale's value indicates the number of clock ticks that will occur in a microsecond. When the processor speed is set to 1MHz, the Time Scale is set to 1.

The current value of Time Scale is accessible via a read-only register in the Bus Register Area. [Section 4.2].

4.1.2 Time of Day Clock (TOD)

The TOD clock is a read-only doubleword value set by μMPS3 circuitry to zero at system boot/reset time. It is incremented by one after every processor cycle; i.e. a clock tick. Each μMPS3 machine instruction is designed to take one processor cycle to execute. Successive readings of the TOD clock can be used to measure time spans. Access to the TOD clock requires the processor to be in kernel-mode, otherwise an Address Error Program Trap exception is raised.

Access to the TOD clock value can be accomplished either of the following ways:

- Direct access to the Bus Register memory location: 0x1000.001C

- Appendix C contains a listing of the μMPS3 System-wide constants file contst.h. Included in this file is a pre-defined macro STCK(T) which takes an unsigned integer as its input parameter and populates it with the value of the low-order word of the TOD clock divided by the Time Scale. [Section 4.1.1]

Important Point: The TOD clock does not generate interrupts. It is set to zero at system boot/reset time and begins counting up by one after each clock cycle.

4.1.3 Interval Timer

The single system-wide Interval Timer is a 32-bit unsigned value that is decremented by one every processor cycle. The μMPS3 circuitry automatically sets the Interval Timer to 0xFFFF.FFFF at system boot/reset time. The Interval Time generates an interrupt on line 2 whenever it makes the 0x0000.0000 $\Rightarrow$ 0xFFFF.FFFF transition.

Access (read or write) to the Interval Timer requires the processor to be in kernel-mode, otherwise an Address Error Program Trap exception is raised.

The Interval Timer is the only device attached to interrupt line 2, hence all interrupts on this line are associated with the Interval Timer.

Interval Timer interrupts are acknowledged by writing a new value into the Interval Timer register.

Access to the Interval Timer can be accomplished either of the following ways:

- Direct access to the Bus Register memory location: 0x1000.0020

- Appendix C contains a listing of the μMPS3 System-wide constants file contst.h. Included in this file is a pre-defined macro LDIT(T) which loads the Interval Timer with the value T (unsigned int) multiplied by the Time Scale value. [Section 4.1.1]

4.1.4 Processor Local Timer (PLT)

Similar in behavior to the Interval Timer is the Processor Local Timer (PLT). Each processor, implemented as part of its **CP0** coprocessor, has its own independent local timer. Unlike the TOD clock and the Interval Timer, each PLT is implemented using a special **CP0 Timer** register. Hence there is no field for PLTs in the Bus Register Area.

The **CP0 Timer** register is decremented by one every processor clock cycle. A PLT will generate an interrupt on interrupt line 1 whenever it makes the 0x0000.0000 $\Rightarrow$ 0xFFFF.FFFF transition.

A PLT is the only device attached to interrupt line 1, hence all interrupts on this line are associated with the PLT. PLT interrupts are acknowledged by writing a new value into the **CP0 Timer** register.

Unlike the Interval Timer, a PLT can be enabled/disabled. Whether this timer is enabled or not is determined by the **Status.TE** (Timer Enable) bit. When **Status.TE**=0 the PLT will neither decrement nor generate interrupts. Only an enabled PLT can generate interrupts. When a pending PLT (line 1) interrupt actually triggers an interrupt is still controlled by the **Status.IEc** and **Status.IM**. [Section 2.3]

Since the PLT is a **CP0** register, access is the same as any other **CP0** register. For **Timer** one uses the libumps functions: setTIMER() and getTIMER() [Section 7.1]

Important Point: The Interval Timer and the PLTs both count down, while the TOD clock counts up. The TOD clock cannot generate an interrupt while both the

Interval Timer (interrupt line 2) and the PLTs (interrupt line 1) can each generate interrupts.

Important Point: Since there is never any ambiguity regarding a line 1 or line 2 interrupt, there is no corresponding Interrupting Devices Bit Map for these interrupt lines.

4.2   Bus Register Area

The bus register area is an eleven word area allocated in **kseg0** (BIOS Region) containing

Physical Address	Field Name
0x1000.0028	TLB Floor Address
0x1000.0024	Time Scale
0x1000.0020	Interval Timer
0x1000.001C	Time of Day Clock - Low
0x1000.0018	Time of Day Clock - High
0x1000.0014	Installed Bootstrap BIOS Size
0x1000.0010	Bootstrap BIOS Base Physical Address
0x1000.000C	Installed Exec. BIOS Size
0x1000.0008	Exec. BIOS Base Physical Address
0x1000.0004	Installed RAM Size
0x1000.0000	RAM Base Physical Address

Table 4.1: Bus Register Area

The first six words/fields are read-only and are set at system boot/reset time. RAMTOP is calculated by adding the RAM base physical address (fixed at 0x2000.0000) to the installed RAM size. EXECTOP (Exec. BIOS Base addr + Exec. BIOS size) and BOOTTOP (Bootstrap BIOS Base addr + Bootstrap BIOS size) are calculated in similar fashion.

The other five words are:

1. Time Scale: [Section 4.1.1]

2. Time of Day Clock (TOD): The read-only double-word register, split into its high and low components, that is the TOD clock. [Section 4.1.2]

3. Interval Timer: The read/writable unsigned register that is the Interval Timer. [Section 4.1.3]

4. TLB Floor Address: This is the threshold below which address translation is disabled and the logical address is the physical address. [Section 6.3.1] The TLB Floor Address is a user configurable value set via the μMPS3 Machine Configuration Panel. [Section 12.2.1]

Appendix A contains a C-language struct definition for the Bus Register area.

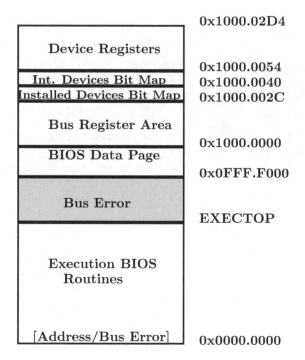

Figure 4.1: Bus Register Area Location

Television is a device that permits people who haven't anything to do to watch people who can't do anything.

Fred Allen

5

Peripheral Devices

μMPS3 supports five different classes of peripheral devices: disk, flash, network card, printer and terminal. Furthermore, μMPS3 can support up to eight instances of each device type. Each single device is operated by a *controller*. Controllers exchange information with the processor via *device registers*: special (**kseg0**) memory locations.

A device register is a consecutive 4-word block of memory. By writing and reading specific fields in a given device register, the processor may both issue commands, test device status, and obtain data results.

μMPS3 implements the *full-handshake interrupt-driven* protocol. Specifically:

1. Communication with device i is initiated by the writing of a command code into device i's device register.

2. Device i's controller responds by both starting the indicated operation and setting a status field in i's device register.

3. When the indicated operation completes, device i's controller will again set some fields in i's device register; including the status field. Furthermore, device i's controller will generate an interrupt exception by asserting the appropriate interrupt line. The generated interrupt exception informs the

25

processor that the requested operation has concluded and that the device requires its attention.

4. The interrupt is acknowledged by writing the acknowledge command code in device i's device register.

5. Device i's controller will de-assert the interrupt line and the protocol can restart. For performance purposes, writing a new command after the interrupt is generated will both acknowledge the interrupt and start a new operation immediately.

The device registers are located in low-memory starting at 0x1000.0054. Since this area falls in **kseg0**, all references are considered physical addresses and access is limited to kernel mode (**Status.KUc=0**). [Chapter 6]

The following table details the correspondence between device class/type and interrupt line.

Interrupt Line #	Device Class
0	Inter-processor interrupts
1	Processor Local Timer
2	Interval Timer (Bus)
3	Disk Devices
4	Flash Devices
5	Network (Ethernet) Devices
6	Printer Devices
7	Terminal Devices

Table 5.1: Interrupt Line and Device Class Mapping

Some important issues relating to device management:

• Since there are multiple interrupt lines, and multiple devices attached to the same interrupt line, at any point in time there may be multiple interrupts pending simultaneously; both across interrupt lines and on the same interrupt line.

• The lower the interrupt line number, the higher the priority of the interrupt. Note how fast/critical devices (e.g. disk devices) are attached to a high priority interrupt line while slow devices are attached to the low priority interrupt lines.

- Interrupt lines 3–7 are used for peripheral devices.

- Interrupt line 0 is for inter-processor interrupts coordination. [Section 9.4]

- Interrupt line 1 is reserved for PLT interrupts. [Section 4.1.4]

- Interrupt line 2 is reserved for the system-wide Interval Timer. [Section 4.1.3]

- Disk and flash devices support *Direct Memory Access* (DMA); that is through cooperation with the bus, these devices are able to transfer whole blocks of data to/from memory from/to the device. Data blocks must be both word-aligned and of multiple-word in size. μMPS3 supports any number of concurrent DMA operations; each on a different device. Care must be taken to prevent simultaneous DMA operations on the same chunk of memory.

- After an operation has begun on a device, its device register "freezes" – becomes read-only – and will not accept any other commands until the operation completes.

- Any device register for an uninstalled device is "frozen" – set to zero – and subsequent writes to the device register have no effect.

- Device registers use only physical addresses; this includes addresses used in DMA operations.

- Each external device in μMPS3 is identified by the interrupt line it is attached to and its device number; an integer in [0..7]. μMPS3 limits the number of devices per interrupt line to eight.

- For performance reasons, devices in the same class are, by default, attached to the same interrupt line.

5.1 Device Registers

All external devices share the same device register structure.

While each device class has a specific use and format for these fields, all device classes, except terminal devices, use:

- **COMMAND** to allow commands to be issued to the device controller.

- **STATUS** for the device controller to communicate the device status to the processor.

- **DATA0** & **DATA1** to pass additional parameters to the device controller or the passing of data from the device controller.

Field #	Address	Field Name
3	(base) + 0xc	**DATA1**
2	(base) + 0x8	**DATA0**
1	(base) + 0x4	**COMMAND**
0	(base) + 0x0	**STATUS**

Table 5.2: Device Register Layout

All 40 device registers in μMPS3 are located in low memory starting at 0x1000.0054. Immediately before the device registers are two other data structures:

- *Installed Devices Bit Map*: A five word structure located at 0x1000.002C indicating which devices are actually installed.

- *Interrupting Devices Bit Map*: A five word structure located at 0x1000.0040 indicating which devices have an interrupt pending.

Given an interrupt line (IntLineNo) and a device number (DevNo) one can compute the starting address of the device's device register:
devAddrBase = 0x1000.0054 + ((IntlineNo - 3) * 0x80) + (DevNo * 0x10)

Appendix A contains C-language struct definitions for an individual device register and the collection of devices registers.

5.2   Device Bit Maps

5.2.1   Installed Devices Bit Map

This is a read-only five word area that indicates which devices are attached to which interrupt line. One word each is reserved to describe the devices attached to interrupt lines 3–7.

Word #	Physical Address	Field Name
4	0x1000.002C + 0x10	Interrupt Line 7 Installed Devices Bit Map
3	0x1000.002C + 0x0C	Interrupt Line 6 Installed Devices Bit Map
2	0x1000.002C + 0x08	Interrupt Line 5 Installed Devices Bit Map
1	0x1000.002C + 0x04	Interrupt Line 4 Installed Devices Bit Map
0	0x1000.002C	Interrupt Line 3 Installed Devices Bit Map

Table 5.3: Installed Devices Bit Map Addresses

Each Installed Devices Bit Map word has the same format:

Figure 5.1: Installed Devices Bit Map Word

When bit i in word j is set to one then there is a device, with device number i that is attached to interrupt line $j + 3$. These words are set by μMPS3 at system boot/reset time and never change.

5.2.2 Interrupting Devices Bit Map

This is a read-only five word area that indicates which devices have an interrupt pending. One word each is reserved to indicate which devices have interrupts pending on interrupt lines 3–7.

Interrupting Devices Bit Map words have the same format as Installed Device Bit Map words. When bit i in word j is set to one then device i attached to interrupt line $j + 3$ has a pending interrupt. [Figure 5.1]

An interrupt pending bit is turned on automatically by the hardware whenever a device's controller asserts the interrupt line to which it is attached. The interrupt will remain pending –the pending interrupt bit will remain on– until the interrupt is acknowledged. Interrupts for peripheral devices are acknowledged by writing the acknowledge command code in the appropriate device's device register.

Word #	Physical Address	Field Name
4	0x1000.0040 + 0x10	Interrupt Line 7 Interrupting Devices Bit Map
3	0x1000.0040 + 0x0C	Interrupt Line 6 Interrupting Devices Bit Map
2	0x1000.0040 + 0x08	Interrupt Line 5 Interrupting Devices Bit Map
1	0x1000.0040 + 0x04	Interrupt Line 4 Interrupting Devices Bit Map
0	0x1000.0040	Interrupt Line 3 Interrupting Devices Bit Map

Table 5.4: Interrupting Devices Bit Map Addresses

Whenever any of the devices on interrupt line i has an interrupt pending, in addition to the interrupt pending bit(s) in the $i - 3$rd word of the Interrupting Devices Bit Map being on, **Cause.IP**[i] will also be on. **Cause.IP**[i] will only be off when none of the devices attached to line i have a pending interrupt.

Interrupt pending bits, both in **Cause.IP** and in the Interrupting Devices Bit Map get automatically turned on in response to device controllers asserting interrupt lines. The interrupt masking flags, **Status.IEc** and **Status.IM**, are used to determine if a pending interrupt actually generates an interrupt exception or not. A pending interrupt on interrupt line i will generate an interrupt exception if both **Status.IEc** and **Status.IM**[i] are set to 1.

Important Point: Many interrupt lines may be active at the same time. Furthermore, many devices on the same interrupt line may be requesting service. **Cause.IP** and the Interrupting Devices Bit Map are always up to date, immediately responding to external device events.

Appendix A contains a C-language struct definition for the Installed Device Bit Map and Interrupting Devices Bit Map.

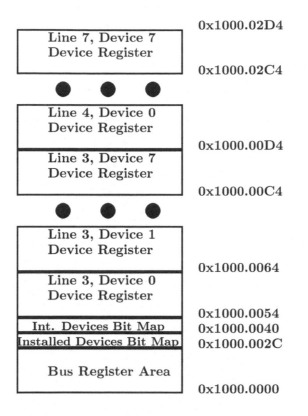

Figure 5.2: Device Registers Area

5.3 Disk Devices

μMPS3 supports up to eight DMA supporting read/writable hard disk drive devices. All μMPS3 disk drives have a sector/block size equal to the μMPS3 framesize of 4KB. Each installed disk drive's device register **DATA1** field is read-only and describes the physical characteristics of the device's geometry.

31	16 15	8 7	0
MAXCYL	MAXHEAD	MAXSECT	

Figure 5.3: Disk Device **DATA1** Field

μMPS3 disk drives can have up to 65536 cylinders/track, addressed [0..**MAXCYL**-1]; 256 heads (or track surfaces), addressed [0..**MAXHEAD**-1]; and 256 sectors/track, addressed [0..**MAXSECT**-1]. Each 4 KB physical disk block (or sector) can be addressed by specifying its coordinates: (cyl, head, sect).

A disk drive **STATUS** field is read-only and will contain one of the following status codes:

Code	Status	Possible Reason for Code
0	Device Not Installed	Device not installed
1	Device Ready	Device waiting for a command
2	Illegal Operation Code Error	Device presented unknown command
3	Device Busy	Device executing a command
4	Seek Error	Illegal parameter/hardware failure
5	Read Error	Illegal parameter/hardware failure
6	Write Error	Illegal parameter/hardware failure
7	DMA Transfer Error	Illegal physical address/hardware failure

Table 5.5: Disk Drive Status Codes

Status codes 1, 2, and 4–7 are completion codes. An illegal parameter may be an out of bounds value (e.g. a cylinder number outside of [0..(**MAXCYL**-1)]), or a non-existent physical address for DMA transfers.

A disk drive **DATA0** device register field is read/writable and is used to specify the starting physical address for a read or write DMA operation. Since memory is addressed from low addresses to high, this address is the lowest word-aligned physical address of the 4 KB block about to be transferred.

A disk drive **COMMAND** field is read/writable and is used to issue commands to the disk drive.

Code	Command	Operation
0	RESET	Reset the device and move the boom to cylinder 0
1	ACK	Acknowledge a pending interrupt
2	SEEKCYL	Seek to the specified **CYLNUM**
3	READBLK	Copy the block located at (**HEADNUM, SECTNUM**) in the current cylinder into RAM at the address in **DATA0**
4	WRITEBLK	Copy the 4 KB of RAM at the address in **DATA0** onto the block located at (**HEADNUM, SECTNUM**) in the current cylinder

Table 5.6: Disk Drive Command Codes

The format of the **COMMAND** register, as illustrated in Figure 5.4, differs depending on which command is to be issued:

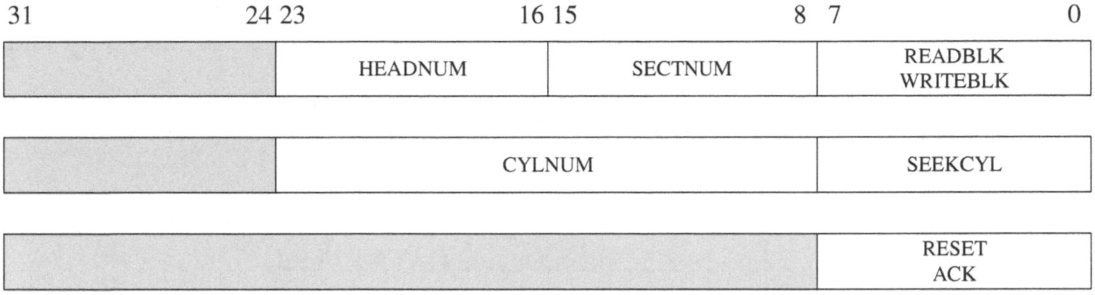

31	24 23	16 15	8 7	0
	HEADNUM	SECTNUM	READBLK WRITEBLK	

		CYLNUM	SEEKCYL

	RESET ACK

Figure 5.4: Disk Device **COMMAND** Field

A disk operation is started by loading the appropriate value into the **COMMAND** field. For the duration of the operation the device's status is "Device Busy." Upon completion of the operation an interrupt is raised and an appropriate status code is set; "Device Ready" for successful completion or one of the error codes. The interrupt is then acknowledged by issuing an ACK or RESET command.

Disk device performance, because both read and write operations are DMA-based, strongly depends on the system clock speed. While read/write throughput may reach MB's/sec in magnitude, the disk hardware operations remain in the millisecond range.

μMPS3 disk devices must first be created using the umps3-mkdev utility prior to use. [Chapter 11]

5.4   Flash Devices

μMPS3 supports up to eight flash-based, DMA supporting, storage devices utilizing a 4 KB blocksize. Each device's register **DATA1** field is read-only and describes the physical characteristics of the device's geometry.

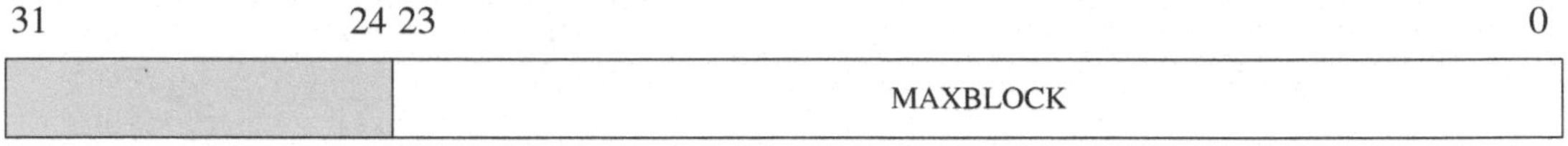

31	24 23	0
	MAXBLOCK	

Figure 5.5: Flash Device **DATA1** Field

μMPS3 flash devices can have up to 2^{24} blocks, addressed [0..**MAXBLOCK**-1]. Each 4 KB block is addressed by specifying its block number.

A flash device **STATUS** field is read-only and will contain one of the following status codes:

Code	Status	Possible Reason for Code
0	Device Not Installed	Device not installed
1	Device Ready	Device waiting for a command
2	Illegal Operation Code Error	Device presented unknown command
3	Device Busy	Device executing a command
4	Read Error	Illegal parameter/hardware failure
5	Write Error	Illegal parameter/hardware failure
6	DMA Transfer Error	Illegal physical address/hardware failure

Table 5.7: Flash Device Status Codes

Status codes 1, 2, and 4–6 are completion codes. An illegal parameter may be an out of bounds value (e.g. a block number outside of [0..(**MAXBLOCK**-1)]), or a non-existent physical address for DMA transfers.

A flash device **DATA0** field is read/writable and is used to specify the starting physical address for a read or write DMA operation. Since memory is addressed from low addresses to high, this address is the lowest word-aligned physical address of the 4 KB block about to be transferred.

A flash device **COMMAND** field is read/writable and is used to issue commands to the device.

Code	Command	Operation
0	RESET	Reset the device interface
1	ACK	Acknowledge a pending interrupt
2	READBLK	Read the block located at (**BLOCKNUMBER**) and copy it into RAM starting at the address in **DATA0**
3	WRITEBLK	Copy the 4 KB of RAM starting at the address in **DATA0** into the block located at (**BLOCKNUMBER**)

Table 5.8: Flash Device Command Codes

The format of the **COMMAND** field, as illustrated in Figure 5.6, differs depending on which command is to be issued:

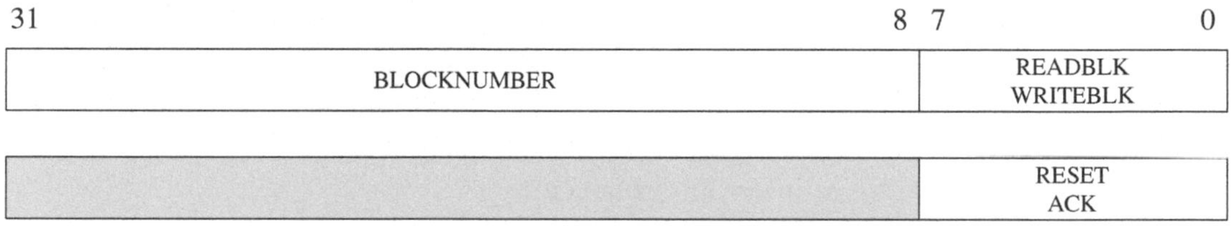

31	8	7	0
BLOCKNUMBER		READBLK WRITEBLK	

		RESET ACK	

Figure 5.6: Flash Device **COMMAND** Field

An operation on a flash device is started by loading the appropriate value into the **COMMAND** field. For the duration of the operation the device's status is "Device Busy." Upon completion of the operation an interrupt is raised and an appropriate status code is set; "Device Ready" for successful completion or one of the error codes. The interrupt is then acknowledged by issuing an ACK or RESET command.

Flash device performance, while somewhat dependent on the system clock speed, remain significantly slower than disk devices. A flash device read (or write) take approximately 15 times longer than a disk seek operation.

μMPS3 flash devices must first be created using the umps3-mkdev utility prior to use. [Chapter 11]

5.5   Network (Ethernet) Adapters

μMPS3 supports up to eight DMA supporting network (i.e. Ethernet) adapters. Though these devices are DMA-based, they are not block devices. Network adapters operate at the byte level and transfer into/out of memory only the amount of data called for. Since packets on a network typically follow standard MTU sizes, this data should never exceed (by much) 1500 bytes.

Network adapters share some characteristics with terminal devices; they are simultaneously both an input device and an output device. As an output device, network adapters behave like other peripherals: a write command is issued and when the write (i.e. transmit) is completed, an interrupt is generated.

For packet receipt, there are two modes of operation:

- Interrupt Enabled: Whenever a packet arrives, an interrupt is generated - this interrupt is not the result of an earlier command. After ACK'ing this interrupt one issues a READNET command to read the packet. When the read is completed, another interrupt is generated, which itself must also be ACK'ed. In Interrupt Enabled mode, each incoming packet, when successfully read, is a two-interrupt sequence.

- Interrupt Disabled: When packets arrive, no interrupt is generated. The network adapter must be polled to determine if a packet is available. The READNET command is non-blocking, and returns 0 if there is no packet to be read. The READNET command will still generate an interrupt, which must be ACK'ed, upon its conclusion.

A network adapter **STATUS** device register field is read-only and will contain one of the following status codes:

Status codes 1, 2, and 5–7 are completion codes. An illegal address may be an out of bounds value or a non-existent physical address for DMA transfers.

Status code 128 is not a distinct status code, it is used in a logical OR fashion with the other status codes. Hence there are actually thirteen status values: 0, (1 & 129), (2 & 130),..., (7 & 135). For example, a status code value of 130 indicates that both an illegal operation was requested AND there is a packet pending for reading. The Read Pending status codes are only used when the network adapter is operating Interrupt Enable mode.

A network adapter **COMMAND** device register field is read/writable and is used to issue commands to the network adapter.

Code	Status	Possible Reason for Code
0	Device Not Installed	Device not installed
1	Device Ready	Device waiting for a command
2	Illegal Operation Code Error	Device presented unknown command
3	Device Busy	Device executing a command
5	Read Error	Error reading packet from device
6	Write Error	Error attempt to send packet
7	DMA Transfer Error	Illegal physical address/hardware failure
128	Read Pending	Interrupts Enabled and packet present

Table 5.9: Network Adapter Status Codes

Code	Command	Operation
0	RESET	Reset the device and reset all configuration data to defaults
1	ACK	Acknowledge a pending interrupt
2	READCONF	Read configuration data into **DATA0** & **DATA1**
3	READNET	Read the next packet from the adapter and copy it into RAM starting at the address in **DATA0**
4	WRITENET	Send a packet of data starting at the RAM address in **DATA0**, whose length is in **DATA1**
5	CONFIG	Update adapter configuration data from values in **DATA0** & **DATA1**

Table 5.10: Network Adapter Command Codes

The **DATA0** fields, during configuration operations (READCONF & CONFIG), are defined as follows:

- **ND** (NAMED, bit 8): When **DATA0.ND**=1, the network adapter will automatically fill all outgoing packets' source MAC address field with the network adapter's MAC address.

- **IE** (Interrupt Enable, bit 9): If **DATA0.IE**=1, whenever a packet is pending on the device (i.e. waiting to be read), it will immediately generate an interrupt. After ACK'ing this interrupt, one issues a READNET command

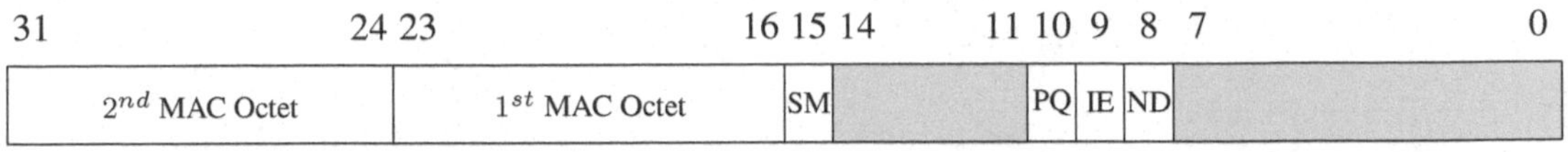

31   24 23   16 15 14   11 10 9 8 7   0
2nd MAC Octet | 1st MAC Octet | SM | | PQ | IE | ND |

Figure 5.7: Network Adapter **DATA0** Field

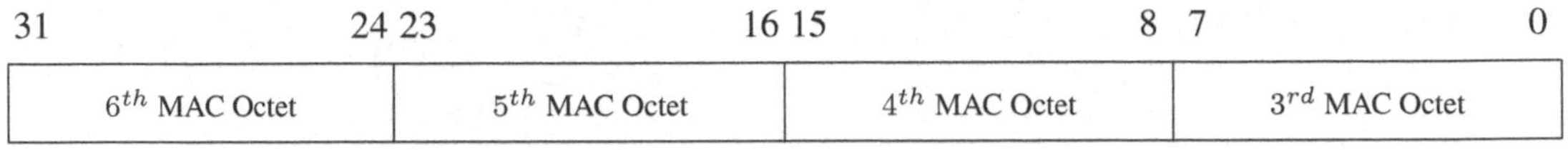

31   24 23   16 15   8 7   0
6th MAC Octet | 5th MAC Octet | 4th MAC Octet | 3rd MAC Octet

Figure 5.8: Network Adapter **DATA1** Field

to facilitate the reading of the packet. The READNET command must then also be ACK'ed.

- **PQ** (PROMISQ, bit 10): If **DATA0.PQ**=1 the network adapter will capture and save all packets its receives. When **DATA0.PQ**=0, the device will ignore/drop any packets not intended for its MAC address. Broadcast packets will still be received even when **DATA0.PQ**=0.

- **SM** (SetMAC, bit 15): When **DATA0.SM**=1 and a CONFIG command is issued, the MAC address of the adapter is updated to the values in **DATA0** & **DATA1**. When **DATA0.sm**=0 and a CONFIG command is issued, the adapter's MAC address remains unchanged.

As described above, the **DATA0** & **DATA1** fields are overloaded; either containing device status values or DMA addresses and lengths. One uses the CONFIG to set network adapter configuration values. Similarly, after a READNET or WRITENET operation, one can use a READCONF operation to reset the **DATA0** & **DATA1** registers to reflect the current adapter configuration values.

5.6 Printer Devices

μMPS3 supports up to eight parallel printer interfaces, each one with a single 8-bit character transmission capability with a maximum throughput of 125 KB/sec.

The **DATA0** field for printer devices is read/writable and is used to set the character to be transmitted to the printer. The character is placed in the low-order byte of the **DATA0** field. The **DATA1** field, for printer devices is not used.

31   8 7   0

| | CHAR |

Figure 5.9: Printer Device **DATA0** Field

A printer **STATUS** field is read-only and will contain one of the following status codes:

Code	Status	Possible Reason for Code
0	Device Not Installed	Device not installed
1	Device Ready	Device waiting for a command
2	Illegal Operation Code Error	Device presented unknown command
3	Device Busy	Device executing a command
4	Print Error	Error during character transmission

Table 5.11: Printer Device Status Codes

Status codes 1, 2, and 4 are completion codes.

A printer **COMMAND** field is read/writable and is used to issue commands to the printer interface.

Code	Command	Operation
0	RESET	Reset the device interface
1	ACK	Acknowledge a pending interrupt
2	PRINTCHR	Transmit the character in **DATA0** over the line

Table 5.12: Printer Device Command Codes

The format of the **COMMAND** field, is illustrated in Figure 5.10.

	COMMAND

Figure 5.10: Printer **COMMAND** Field

A printer operation is started by loading the appropriate value into the **COMMAND** field. For the duration of the operation the device's status is "Device Busy." Upon completion of the operation an interrupt is raised and an appropriate status code is set; "Device Ready" for successful completion or one of the error codes. The interrupt is then acknowledged by issuing an ACK or RESET command.

5.7 Terminal Devices

μMPS3 supports up to eight serial terminal device interfaces, each one with a single 8-bit character transmission and receipt capability.

Each terminal interface contains two sub-devices; a *transmitter* and a *receiver*. These two sub-devices operate independently and concurrently. To support the two-subdevices a terminal interface's device register is redefined as follows:

Field #	Address	Field Name
3	(base) + 0xc	**TRANSM_COMMAND**
2	(base) + 0x8	**TRANSM_STATUS**
1	(base) + 0x4	**RECV_COMMAND**
0	(base) + 0x0	**RECV_STATUS**

Table 5.13: Terminal Device Register Layout

The **TRANSM_STATUS** and **RECV_STATUS** fields (device register fields 0 & 2) are read-only and have the following format.

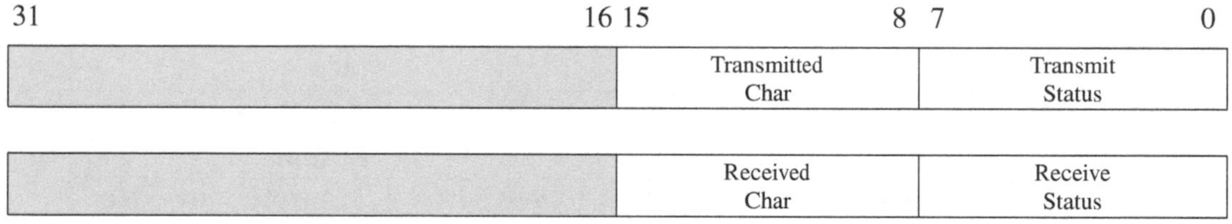

Figure 5.11: Terminal Device **TRANSM_STATUS** and **RECV_STATUS** Fields

The **status** byte has the following meaning:

The meaning of status codes 0–4 are the same as with other device types. Furthermore:

- The Character Received code (5) is set when a character is correctly received from the terminal and is placed in **RECV_STATUS.RECV'D-CHAR**.

- The Character Transmitted code (5) is set when a character is correctly transmitted to the terminal and is placed in **TRANSM_STATUS.TRANS'D-CHAR**.

Code	RECV_STATUS	TRANSM_STATUS
0	Device Not Installed	Device not installed
1	Device Ready	Device Ready
2	Illegal Operation Code Error	Illegal Operation Code Error
3	Device Busy	Device Busy
4	Receive Error	Transmission Error
5	Character Received	Character Transmitted

Table 5.14: Terminal Device Status Codes

- The Device Ready code (1) is set as a response to an ACK or RESET command.

The terminal **TRANSM_COMMAND** and **RECV_COMMAND** fields are read/writable and are used to issue commands to the terminal's interface.

Code	TRANSM COMMAND	RECV COMMAND	Operation
0	RESET	RESET	Reset the transmitter or receiver interface
1	ACK	ACK	Ack a pending interrupt
2	TRANSMITCHAR	RECEIVECHAR	Transmit or Receive the character over the line

Table 5.15: Terminal Device Command Codes

The **TRANSM_COMMAND** and **RECV_COMMAND** fields have the following format:

RECV_COMMAND.RECV-CMD is simply the command.

The **TRANSM_COMMAND** field has two parts

- The command itself: **TRANSM_COMMAND.TRANSM-CMD**

- The character to be transmitted: **TRANSM_COMMAND.TRANSM-CHAR**

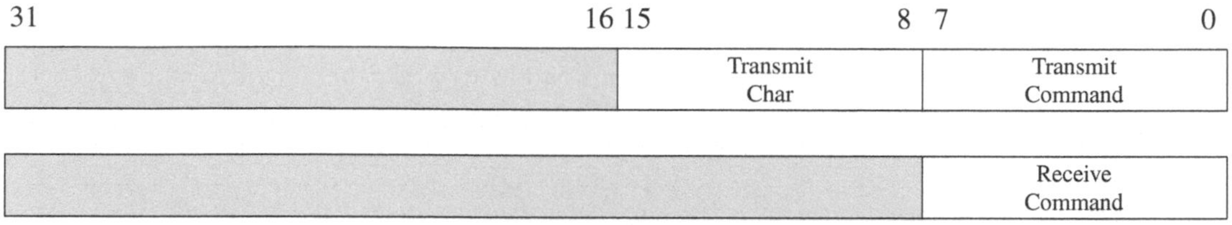

31	16	15	8	7	0
		Transmit Char		Transmit Command	

31	15	8	7	0
			Receive Command	

Figure 5.12: Terminal **TRANSM_COMMAND** and **RECV_COMMAND** Fields

A character is received, and placed in **RECV_STATUS.RECV'D-CHAR** only after a RECEIVECHAR command has been issued to the receiver.

The operation of a terminal device is more complicated than other devices because it is two sub-devices sharing the same device register interface. When a terminal device generates an interrupt, the (operating system's) terminal device interrupt handler, after determining which terminal generated the interrupt, must furthermore determine if the interrupt is for receiving a character, for transmitting a character, or both; i.e. two interrupts pending simultaneously.

If there are two interrupts pending simultaneously, both must be acknowledged in order to have the appropriate interrupt pending bit in the Interrupt Line 7 Interrupting Devices Bit Map turned off.

To make it possible to determine which sub-device has a pending interrupt there are two sub-device "ready" conditions; Device Ready and Character Received/Transmitted. While other device types can use a Device Ready code to signal a successful completion, this is insufficient for terminal devices. For terminal devices it is necessary to distinguish between a state of successful completion though the interrupt is not yet acknowledged, Character Received/Transmitted, and a command whose completion has been acknowledged, Device Ready.

A terminal operation is started by loading the appropriate value(s) into the **TRANSM_COMMAND** or **RECV_COMMAND** field. For the duration of the operation the sub-device's status is "Device Busy." Upon completion of the operation an interrupt is raised and an appropriate status code is set in **TRANSM_STATUS** or **RECV_STATUS** respectively; "Character Transmitted/Received" for successful completion or one of the error codes. The interrupt is acknowledged by issuing an ACK or RESET command to which the sub-device responds by setting the Device Ready code in the respective status field.

The terminal interface's maximum throughput is 12.5 KB/sec for both character transmission and receipt.

Memory is like an orgasm. It's a lot better if you don't have to fake it.

Seymore Cray – on virtual memory

Memory Management

μMPS3 uses 32-bit addresses, giving rise to a 2^{32} byte (4 Gb) address space.

The address space, both physical and logical, is divided into equal sized units of 4 KB each. Hence an address has two components; a 20-bit *Frame Number* (physical) or *Page Number* (logical), and a 12-bit *Offset* into the page. Addresses have the following format:

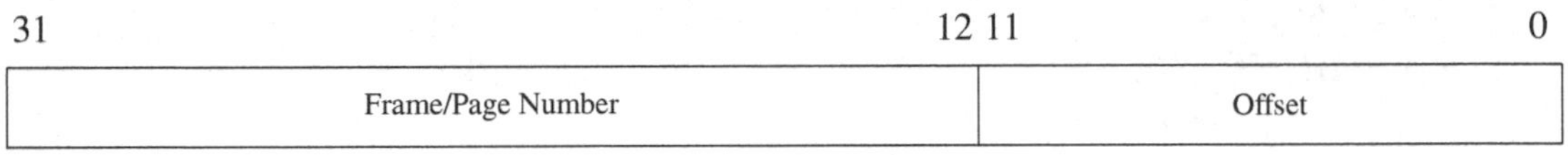

31	12 11	0
Frame/Page Number		Offset

Figure 6.1: Address Format

The 20-bit frame number is either the physical frame number in RAM, or a logical page number which must undergo address translation to determine the actual physical frame number containing the indicated page.

There are two perspectives necessary to understanding memory management in μMPS3: physical and conceptual.

6.1 The Physical View of Memory

Physical memory in μMPS3 is divided into two components: The BIOS portion and RAM.

6.1.1 The BIOS Region of Physical Memory

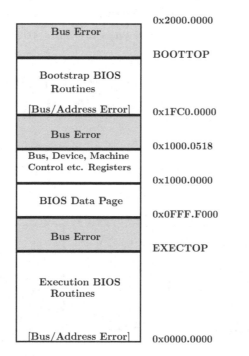

Figure 6.2: Layout of the BIOS Region (**kseg0**)

This 0.5 Gb region is μMPS3's Programmable ROM. It is not strictly ROM memory since:

- It can be "reprogrammed" by supplying different execution time or boot-strap BIOS object files via the μMPS3 Machine Configuration Panel. [Chapter 8]

- The BIOS Data Page is fully read-writable. [Section 8.5]

- The device registers, some bus register fields and the Machine Control registers, Processor Interface registers, and Interrupt Routing table are also writable.

Appendix D contains a more detailed diagram of the BIOS region.
Another name for this region is **kseg0**. [Section 6.2]

Access to this region is limited to kernel-mode only, and then only to the
"accessible" regions: the BIOS Data Page, bus register, device registers, Machine
Control registers, Processor Interface registers, and the Interrupt Routing table.
Kernel-mode access to any undefined or inaccessible portions of the BIOS region
will raise a Bus Error Program Trap exception.

User-mode access to **kseg0** will always raise an Address Error Program Trap
exception.

<u>**Technical Point:**</u> Access to an undefined portion of the BIOS region in user-mode
generates an Address Error exception, since the user-mode access to violation is
checked first.

6.1.2   RAM

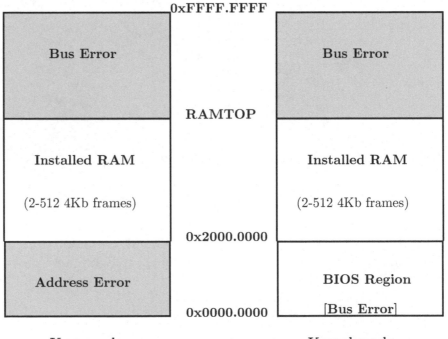

Figure 6.3: Physical Memory

"Installed" RAM starts at 0x2000.0000. The μMPS3 Machine Configuration Panel allows between 8 and 512 frames of RAM. [Section 12.2.1]
This translates to a RAM size ranging from 32 KB up to 2 MB. While 2 MB may feel inadequately small by today's standards, it is more than sufficient for the kinds of projects μMPS3 was created to support: a student-created, experimental, operating system along with all its supporting data structures, plus a sufficiently large frame pool to support virtual address translation.

Hence RAMTOP will range from 0x2000.8000 to 0x2020.0000.

When μMPS3 is started, the RAM Base Physical Address Bus Register (located at 0x1000.0000) is set to 0x2000.0000. The Installed RAM Size Bus Register (located at 0x1000.0004) is set to the number of frames set in the μMPS3 Machine Configuration Panel multiplied by 4 KB. Adding these two values together determines RAMTOP. [Section 4.2]

Any attempt to access a RAM address past RAMTOP will raise a Bus Error Program Trap exception.

6.2 The Conceptual View: The Address Space

The 4 GB address space is logically divided into four chunks/spaces as follows:

- **kseg0** (0x0000.0000 - 0x2000.0000): This 0.5 GB section is the "installed EPROM" BIOS memory region. **kseg0** holds the BIOS routines, device registers, bus device registers, and multiprocessor communication/support structures. [Section 6.1.1]

  This memory section is always present regardless of the amount of installed RAM. Access to **kseg0** is limited to kernel-mode only. User-mode access will raise an Address Error Program Trap exception.

  All addresses in **kseg0** are exempt from virtual address translation: all logical **kseg0** addresses are also their physical address.

- **kseg1** (0x2000.0000 - 0x4000.0000): This 0.5 GB section is designed to hold the kernel/OS. Access to **kseg1** is limited to kernel-mode only. User-mode access will raise an Address Error Program Trap exception.

  Important Point: Since RAMTOP will fall between 0x2000.8000 to 0x2020.0000, RAMTOP is an address in **kseg1**.

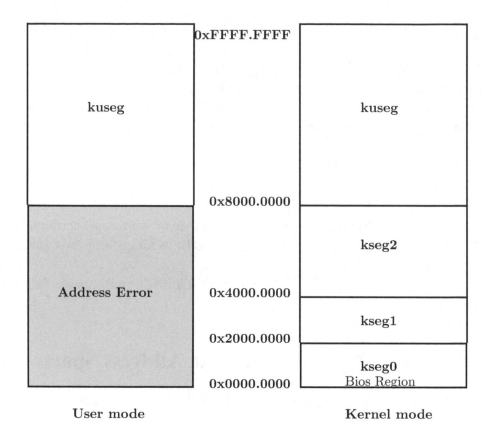

Figure 6.4: Logical Address Space

All addresses in **kseg1** below RAMTOP are exempt from virtual address translation: these logical **kseg1** addresses are also their physical address.

Addresses in **kseg1** above RAMTOP can only be accessible through virtual address translation. Whenever an OS wishes to make use of **kseg1** above RAMTOP, the TLB Floor Address must be set to RAMTOP. Any other setting of TLB Floor Address will not work/is illogical.

- **kseg2** (0x4000.0000 - 0x8000.0000): This 1 GB section is for use when implementing a sophisticated operating system. Access to **kseg2** is limited to kernel-mode only. User-mode access will raise an Address Error Program Trap exception.

  Addresses in **kseg2** can only be accessible through virtual address translation - all **kseg2** addresses are therefore logical. μMPS3 does not permit one to "install" a sufficient quantity of physical RAM so that any logical **kseg2** address is also its physical address. This implies that whenever an OS wishes to make use of **kseg2**, the TLB Floor Address must be set to an address below 0x4000.0000(0x4000.0000 or RAMTOP). Any other setting of TLB Floor Address will not work/is illogical.

* **kuseg** (0x8000.0000- 0xFFFF.FFFF): This 2 GB section is for user programs. Access to **kuseg** is possible from both the kernel-mode and user-mode processor setting.

    Addresses in **kuseg** can only be accessible through virtual address translation - all **kuseg** addresses are therefore logical. μMPS3 does not permit one to "install" a sufficient quantity of physical RAM so that any logical **kuseg** address is also its physical address. This implies that whenever an OS wishes to make use of **kuseg**, the TLB Floor Address must be set to an address below 0x8000.0000(0x8000.0000, 0x4000.0000, or RAMTOP). Any other setting of TLB Floor Address will not work/is illogical.

    The **kuseg** of one process is differentiated from another process's **kuseg** by a unique 6-bit process identifier called the *Address Space Identifier* - **ASID**. The **ASID** is contained in the **EntryHi** register (**EntryHi.ASID**), which is part of a processor state. [Section 2.2]

6.3   Virtual Address Translation in μMPS3

Mapping a logical address to a physical address (address translation) is performed by the *MMU* (Memory Management Unit) of each processor's **CP0** co-processor. **CP0** contains five control registers (**Index**, **Random**, **EntryHi**, **EntryLo**, and **BadVAddr**) in addition to a TLB associative cache to support address translation.

6.3.1   The TLB Floor Address

The TLB Floor Address is an address (RAMTOP, 0x4000.0000, 0x8000.0000, or VM Off) below which address translation is disabled and the address is considered a physical address. Any logical address below the TLB Floor Address is also its physical address. Any address above the TLB Floor Address will undergo an MMU address translation.

The value of the TLB Floor Address is a user configurable value set via the μMPS3 Machine Configuration Panel. [Chapter 12]

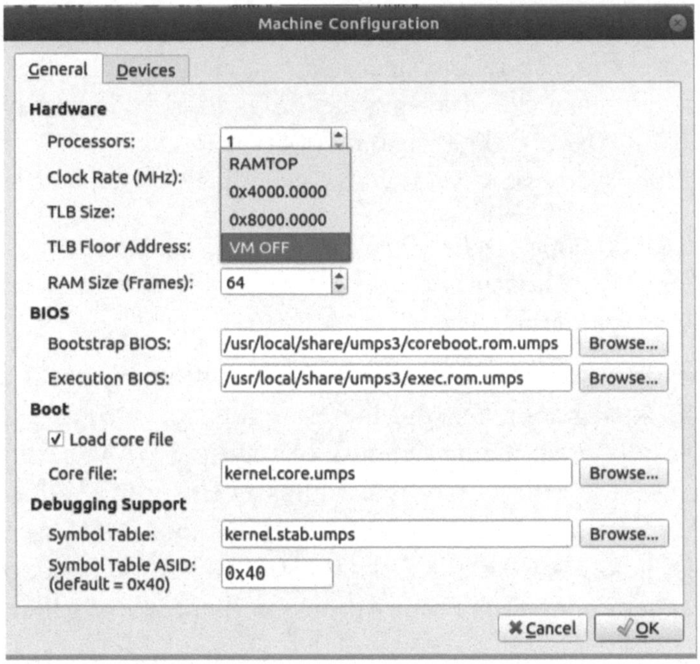

Figure 6.5: TLB Floor Address Configuration Panel

A configurable TLB Floor Address allows μMPS3 to behave differently according to one's needs. The options for TLB Floor Address are:

- VM Off – Address translation is turned off. All addresses are physical addresses.

- 0x8000.0000: Address translation is disabled for the three kernel spaces. All **kuseg** logical addresses undergo MMU address translation to calculate their physical address.

- 0x4000.0000: Address translation is disabled for **kseg0** and **kseg1** and enabled for **kseg2** and **kuseg**. MMU address translation is performed for any **kseg2** and **kuseg** logical address. All **kseg0** and **kseg1** logical addresses are physical addresses.

- RAMTOP: Address translation is disabled for **kseg0** and all **kseg1** addresses below RAMTOP. MMU address translation is performed for any logical address greater than RAMTOP. If the logical address also exists as a physical address, then that address is used, otherwise, an MMU address translation is performed.

The TLB Floor Address cannot be changed while μMPS3 is running. The current value of TLB Floor Address is available in read-only form from the Bus Register Area. [Chapter 4.2]

6.3.2 The TLB

The TLB (*Translation Lookaside Buffer*) is an associative cache, that can hold between 4–64 TLB entries. The size of the TLB is a user configurable value set via the μMPS3 Machine Configuration Panel. [Chapter 12]

The TLB size cannot be changed while the machine is running. The current size of the TLB is denoted as **TLBSIZE**.

Each TLB entry describes the mapping between one **ASID**/logical page number pairing and a physical frame number/location in RAM.

A TLB entry is a 64-bit entry broken down into two parts: **EntryHi** and **EntryLo**.

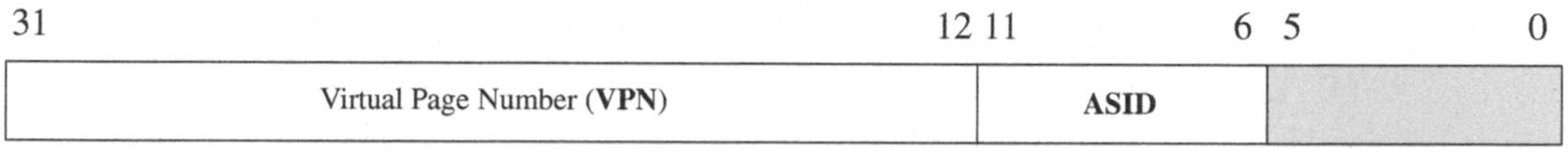

31	12 11	6 5	0
Virtual Page Number (**VPN**)	**ASID**		

Figure 6.6: **EntryHi**

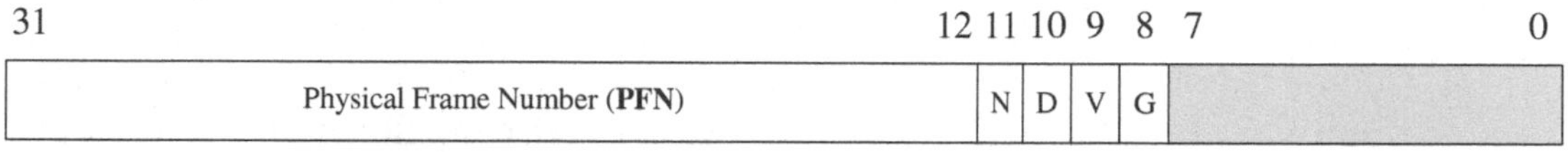

31	12 11 10 9 8 7	0
Physical Frame Number (**PFN**)	N D V G	

Figure 6.7: **EntryLo**

The fields of a TLB entry are defined as follows:

- **VPN** - The virtual page number. This is simply the higher order 20-bits of a logical address. The lower order 12-bits of the address are the offset into a 4 KB (2^{12}) page.

- **ASID** - The Address Space Identifier, a.k.a. process ID for this **VPN**.

- **PFN** - The physical frame number where the **VPN** for the specified **ASID** can be found in RAM.

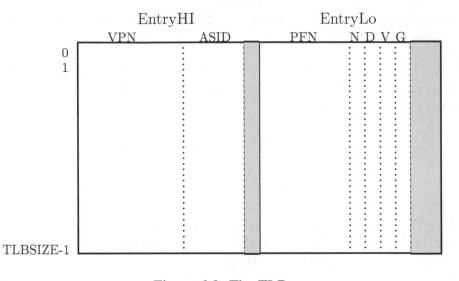

Figure 6.8: The TLB

- **N** - Non-cacheable bit: Not used in μMPS3.

- **D** - Dirty bit: This bit is used to implement memory protection mechanisms. When set to zero (off) a write access to a location in the physical frame will cause a TLB-Modification exception to be raised. This "write protection" bit allows for the realization of memory protection schemes and/or sophisticated page replacement algorithms.

- **V** - Valid bit: If set to 1 (on), this TLB entry is considered valid. A valid entry is one where the **PFN** actually holds the **ASID**/virtual page number pairing. If 0 (off), the indicated **ASID**/virtual page number pairing is not actually in the **PFN** and any access to this page will cause a TLB-Invalid exception to be raised. In practical terms, a TLB-Invalid exception is what is generically called a "page fault."

- **G** - Global bit: If set to 1 (on), the TLB entry will match any **ASID** with the corresponding **VPN**. This bit allows for memory sharing schemes.

Important Point: Each TLB entry is composed of two parts: **EntryHi** and **EntryLo**. Confusingly, there are two **CP0** control registers used by **CP0** during address translation: **EntryHi** and **EntryLo**. These two registers share their names and formats with each TLB entry though they serve different purposes. Unless explicitly stated, all references to **EntryHi** or **EntryLo** refer to the **CP0** registers.

6.3.3 Address Translation in μMPS3

The **ASID** to be used for the translation is the current contents of **EntryHi.ASID**. The logical address to be translated (i.e. any address greater than or equal to TLB Floor Address) is sent to **CP0**.

Logical address to physical address translation proceeds as follows:

1. If the address is below TLB Floor Address, translation ceases. The address is a physical address.

2. If the address to be translated is in **kseg0**, **kseg1**, or **kseg2 and Status.KUc=1** (i.e. User-mode) **BadVAddr** is loaded with the logical address and an Address Error exception is raised. [Section 3.1.1]

3. All TLB entries are "simultaneously" searched for a matching TLB entry.[1] A match is defined as a TLB entry whose **VPN** is the same as that of the logical address being translated, and either the global bit is on (**G**=1) or the **ASID** of the entry matches **EntryHi.ASID**. If more than one TLB entry matches, the highest numbered matching TLB entry is used.

4. If no matching entry is found the logical address being translated is placed in the **CP0 BadVAddr** register, **EntryHi.VPN** is similarly loaded, and a TLB-Refill event is raised. [Section 3.1.1]

5. If a matching TLB entry is found then the entry's **V** and **D** control bits are checked respectively. If no TLB-Invalid or TLB-Modification exception is raised, the physical address is constructed by concatenating the **Offset** from the logical address to be translated to the **PFN** from the matching TLB entry. If a TLB-Invalid or TLB-Modification exception is raised the logical address being translated is placed in the **CP0 BadVAddr** register and **EntryHi.VPN** is similarly loaded by the processor. [Section 3.1.1]

6. Finally, the constructed physical address is checked against two thresholds:

   - If the address is above RAMTOP a Bus Error exception is raised.
   - If the address is below 0x2000.0000 an Address Error exception is raised if **Status.KUc**=1. (i.e. User-mode access to **kseg0**.)

---

[1]μMPS3's associative TLB is emulated via a linear search.

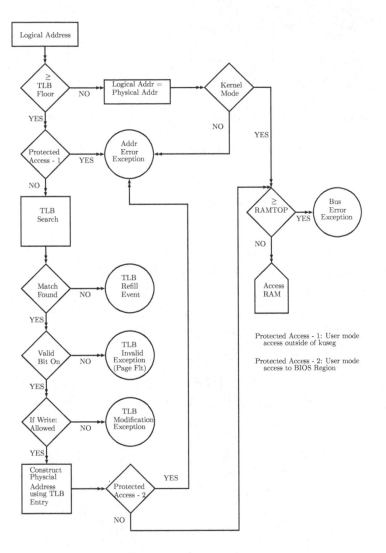

Figure 6.9: Address Translation Flowchart

6.4   CP0 Registers and Instructions for TLB Management

Given the RISC design behind μMPS3, the **CP0** MMU is rather simple/minimal. For each logical address sent to **CP0** for translation the TLB is "associatively" searched. If no match is found, a TLB-Refill event is raised. If a match is found, the **V** and **D** bits are checked, and either an exception is raised (TLB-Invalid or

TLB-Modification) or the translated physical address is constructed.

When a TLB-Refill event occurs, the processor with some assistance from the BIOS-TLB-Refill handler, essentially passes control to a kernel function: hopefully, the kernel TLB-Refill handler. [Chapter 3]
It is the job of this kernel function to locate (in a kernel page table?) or construct an appropriate TLB entry, insert this new TLB entry into the TLB, and restart the instruction.

The same is true on TLB-Invalid and TLB-Modification exceptions. The processor will perform a few key steps and pass control to the BIOS-Excpt handler which in turn will pass control to a different kernel function. [Chapter 3]
At that point, what happens next is up to the kernel. Most likely, the kernel will at least treat TLB-Invalid exceptions as a *Page Fault* and take appropriate action.

For TLB-Refill events, and possibly TLB-Invalid and TLB-Modification exceptions, the kernel will need to access and modify the TLB. To facilitate this there are special **CP0** registers and instructions for this purpose.

CP0 implements five registers used to support virtual address translation.

The contents of the TLB can be modified by writing values into the **CP0 EntryHi** and **EntryLo** registers [Section 7.1] and issuing either the *TLB-Write-Index* (**TLBWI**) or *TLB-Write-Random* (**TLBWR**) **CP0** instruction. [Section 7.2.1]

Which slot in the TLB the entry is written into is determined by which instruction is used and the contents of either the **Random** or **Index CP0** register.

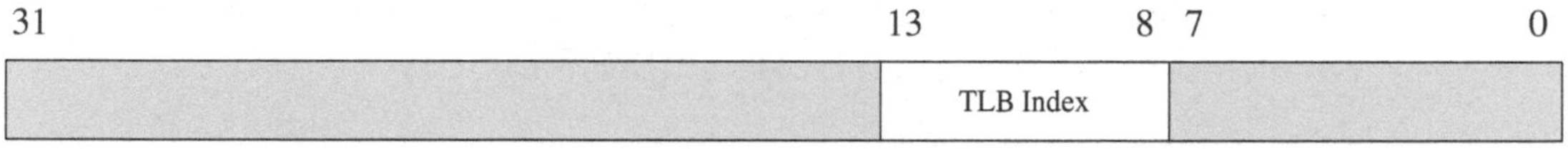

31	13	8	7	0
	TLB Index			

Figure 6.10: **Random CP0** Control Register

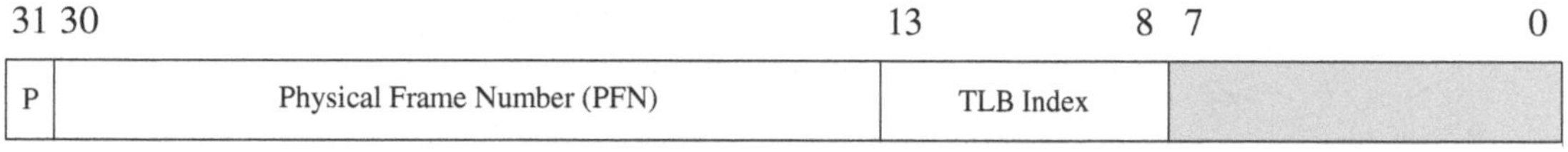

31	30	13	8	7	0
P	Physical Frame Number (PFN)	TLB Index			

Figure 6.11: **Index CP0** Control Register

Both the **Random** and the **Index CP0** registers have a 6-bit **TLB-Index** field which addresses one of the **TLBSIZE** slots in the TLB. The **Index** register is a read/writable register. [Section 7.1] When a **TLBWI** instruction is executed, the contents of the **EntryHi** and **EntryLo CP0** registers are written into the slot indicated by **Index.TLB-Index**.

The **Random** register is a read-only register used to index the TLB randomly; allowing for more effective TLB-refiling schemes. **Random.TLB-Index** is initialized to **TLBSIZE**-1 and is automatically decremented by one every processor cycle until it reaches 1 at which point it starts back again at **TLBSIZE**-1. This leaves one TLB "safe" entry (entry 0) which cannot be indexed by **Random**. When a **TLBWR** instruction is executed, the contents of the **EntryHi** and **EntryLo CP0** registers are written into the TLB slot indicated by **Random.TLB-Index**.

Three other useful **CP0**-related instructions associated with the TLB are the *TLB-Read* (**TLBR**), *TLB-Probe* (**TLBP**), and the *TLB-Clear* (**TLBCLR**) commands.

- The **TLBR** (*TLB-Read*) command places the TLB entry indexed by **Index.TLB-Index** into the **EntryHi** and **EntryLo CP0** registers. [Section 7.2.1]

  Important Point: **TLBR** has the potentially dangerous affect of altering the value of **EntryHi.ASID**.

- The **TLBP** (*TLB-Probe*) command initiates a TLB search for a matching entry in the TLB that matches the current values in the **EntryHi CP0** register. If a matching entry is found in the TLB the corresponding index value is loaded into **Index.TLB-Index** and the Probe bit (**Index.P**) is set to 0. If no match is found, **Index.P** is set to 1. [Section 7.2.1]

- The **TLBCLR** (*TLB-Clear*) command zero's out the "unsafe" TLB entries; entries 1 through **TLBSIZE**-1 This command effectively invalidates the current contents of the TLB cache. [Section 7.3]

TLB Action	TLB Command	C usage	Outcome
Read a TLB Entry	**TLBR**	`void TLBR()`	**EntryHi/EntryLo** ← TLB
Search the TLB	**TLBP**	`void TLBP()`	**Index** ← search result
Write a random TLB Entry	**TLBWR**	`void TLBWR()`	TLB ← **EntryHi/EntryLo**
Write a specific TLB Entry	**TLBWI**	`void TLBWI()`	TLB ← **EntryHi/EntryLo**
Erase ALL TLB Entries	**TLBCLR**	`void TLBCLR()`	TLB invalidated

Table 6.1: Summary of TLB-related Commands

CP0 Register	Access Commands
EntryHi	`getENTRYHI()` & `setENTRYHI()`
EntryLo	`getENTRYLO()` & `setENTRYLO()`
BadVAddr	`getBADVADDR()`
Index	`getINDEX()` & `setINDEX()`
Random	`getRANDOM()`

Table 6.2: Summary of TLB-related **CP0** Registers

I find television very educational. The minute somebody turns it on, I go to the library and read a good book.

Groucho Marx

7

Library Services - `libumps`

μMPS3 is distributed with a library: `libumps`[1]

- `libumps.S` MIPS assembly source file.

- `libumps.o` Assembled object file.

- `libumps.h` C-language header file. Any C-language source file wishing to utilize `libumps` routines must
#include libumps.h

See Appendix B for a reprint of `libumps.h`

In the process of writing a μMPS3 operating system one needs to access various **CP0** registers (e.g. **Status**) and issue specific assembler instructions (e.g. **SYSCALL**). To avoid the need to program in MIPS assembler, `libumps`, via "wrapper" functions, provides C-language access to **CP0** registers, certain MIPS assembly instructions, in addition to defining a few new instructions.

Specifically, the `libumps` functions fall into three broad categories:

---

[1]libumps.S can be found in the *support* file directory. The header file, libumps.h is installed in the *include* file directory. Finally, the object file, libumps.o, which needs to be linked with the other kernel object files to create an executable kernel can be found in the *library* file directory. [Section H.3]

- Since directly accessing **CP0** registers is impossible in C, libumps provides "wrapper" routines to overcome this.

- Since directly invoking MIPS assembly instructions is impossible in C, libumps provides "wrapper" routines to overcome this.

- New instructions to "extend" the MIPS R2/3000 integer instruction set which are particularly useful for kernel authors.

7.1 Accessing CP0 Registers in C

CP0 implements ten control registers. Six of these registers are read/writable, while the other four are read-only.

libumps provides C-language read access to all ten **CP0** registers as parameterless unsigned integer functions. In each case the contents of the specified **CP0** register is returned to the caller. The

C usage	CP0 Register
unsigned int getINDEX()	**Index**
unsigned int getENTRYHI()	**EntryHi**
unsigned int getENTRYLO()	**EntryLo**
unsigned int getSTATUS()	**Status**
unsigned int getTIMER()	**Timer**
unsigned int getPRID()	**PRID**
unsigned int getCAUSE()	**Cause**
unsigned int getRANDOM()	**Random**
unsigned int getEPC()	**EPC**
unsigned int getBADVADDR()	**BadVAddr**

Table 7.1: Control Register Read Commands

libumps provides C-language write access to the six writable registers as single parameter unsigned integer functions. The single parameter is the value to be loaded into the register and the return value is the value in the register after the load operation.

C usage	CP0 Register
`unsigned int setINDEX(unsigned int)`	**Index**
`unsigned int setENTRYHI(unsigned int)`	**EntryHi**
`unsigned int setENTRYLO(unsigned int)`	**EntryLo**
`unsigned int setSTATUS(unsigned int)`	**Status**
`unsigned int setTIMER(unsigned int)`	**Timer**
`unsigned int setCAUSE(unsigned int)`	**Cause**

Table 7.2: Control Register Write Commands

Important Point: setENTRYHI has the potentially dangerous affect of altering the value of **EntryHi.ASID**.

All sixteen of these instructions require the processor to be in kernel-mode or if in user-mode, to have **Status.CU[0]**=1, otherwise a Coprocessor Unusable Program Trap exception is raised.

7.2   Accessing MIPS Assembly in C

libumps provides C-language access to seven MIPS assembly instructions. Four are **CP0**-related while the other three are general MIPS assembly instructions.

7.2.1   TLB-Related MIPS Assembly Instructions

C usage	Instruction Description	MIPS Assembly
`void TLBWR()`	TLB-Write-Random	**TLBWR**
`void TLBWI()`	TLB-Write-Index	**TLBWI**
`void TLBR()`	TLB-Read	**TLBR**
`void TLBP()`	TLB-Probe	**TLBP**

Table 7.3: TLB Commands

These four **CP0**-related instructions are parameter-less void C functions. The write commands (**TLBWI, TLBWR**) modify the TLB, while the Read and Probe commands modify the **EntryHi, EntryLo,** and **Index CP0** registers. [Section 6.4]

Important Point: TLBR has the potentially dangerous affect of altering the value of **EntryHi.ASID**.

All four of these instructions require the processor to be in kernel-mode or if in user-mode, to have **Status.CU[0]**=1, otherwise a Reserved Instruction (RI) Program Trap exception is raised.

`libumps` provides for a fifth TLB-related instruction/service: **TLBCLR**. **TLBCLR** is not a wrapper function for a MIPS assembly instruction. Instead, it is a new `libumps` implemented instruction/service. [Section 7.3.3]

7.2.2   Kernel-Mode MIPS Assembly Instructions

`libumps` provides C-language access to the **WAIT** privileged MIPS instructions.

Upon execution, the processor enters the *Idle* state and ceases instruction execution. The processor resumes execution when an external event (reset or interrupt) is signaled to the processor.

If the processor resumes execution as a result of an unmasked interrupt, the interrupt exception is considered to have occurred at the instruction following the **WAIT** instruction. If the processor resumes execution as a result of a masked interrupt, no interrupt exception occurs (the interrupt is nevertheless still pending), and execution proceeds with the instruction following the **WAIT** instruction.

C usage	Instruction Description	MIPS Assembly
`void WAIT()`	Idle Processor	**WAIT**

Table 7.4: Wait Command

This instruction requires the processor to be in kernel-mode or if in user-mode, to have **Status.CU[0]**=1, otherwise a Reserved Instruction (RI) Program Trap exception is raised.

Technical Point: The **WAIT** instruction is not part of the MIPS R2/3000 ISA, instead it is part of the MIPS32 ISA. **WAIT** is one of only two MIPS32 instructions implemented in μMPS3.

7.2.3   User-Mode MIPS Assembly Instructions

The SYSCALL Instruction

SYSCALL is the MIPS instruction for requesting operating system service. The execution of the **SYSCALL** instruction causes a System Call (Sys) exception to occur. [Chapter 3]

C usage:

```
unsigned int SYSCALL(unsigned int number,
        unsigned int arg1, unsigned int arg2,
        unsigned int arg3)
```

In keeping with the standard MIPS function call protocol,

- `number` is mapped to register **a0**

- `arg1` is mapped to register **a1**

- `arg2` is mapped to register **a2**

- `arg3` is mapped to register **a3**

Upon return from **SYSCALL**, the return value is taken from the contents of register **v0**.

The parameters for **SYSCALL** have no "universal" meaning. Traditionally, `number` is used to indicate which system service is being requested. The other arguments are used to pass along appropriate parameters, depending on `number`.

The Compare and Swap (CAS) Instruction

CAS performs an atomic read-modify-write operation on synchronizable memory locations.

C usage:

```
int CAS(unsigned int *atomic,
        unsigned int ov, unsigned int nv)
```

where `nv` and `ov` are integers, and `atomic` is a pointer to an integer.

This function atomically sets the word pointed to by `atomic` to `nv` if the current value of the word is `ov`. It returns 1 to indicate a successful update and 0 otherwise.

Technical Point: The **CAS** instruction is not part of the MIPS R2/3000 ISA, instead it is part of the MIPS32 ISA. **CAS** is one of only two MIPS32 instructions implemented in μMPS3. Appendix F provides a detailed description of this MIPS32 instruction.

7.3 New libumps Instructions

In addition to providing "wrapper" functions to access various μMPS3 registers and assembly instruction, libumps extends the MIPS R2/3000 integer instruction set with the following services/instructions:

7.3.1 LDST - Load Processor State

Atomically load the processor state with the state located at the supplied *physical* memory location. [Section 2.2]

This service/instruction requires the processor to be in kernel-mode, otherwise a Breakpoint exception is raised.

C usage:
```
void LDST(state_t *statep)
```
where statep is the physical address of the processor state to be loaded.

7.3.2 STST - Store Processor State

Store the current processor state at the supplied *physical* memory location. [Section 2.2]

STST, which is NOT atomic, does not save off the current contents of the **PC**. Instead, 0 is written into the s_pc field of saved state.

This instruction requires the processor to be in kernel-mode or if in user-mode, to have **Status.CU[0]**=1, otherwise a Reserved Instruction (RI) Program Trap exception is raised.

C usage:
```
void STST(state_t *statep)
```
where statep is the physical address where the current processor state is to be stored.

7.3.3 TLBCLR - TLB Clear

This instruction zeros out the "unsafe" TLB entries: entries 1 through **TLBSIZE-1**. This command effectively invalidates the current contents of the TLB cache.

[Section 6.4]

This instruction requires the processor to be in kernel-mode or if in user-mode, to have **Status.CU[0]**=1, otherwise a Reserved Instruction (RI) Program Trap exception is raised.

C usage:

```
void TLBCLR()
```

7.3.4 LDCXT - Load Context (a.k.a. Store State and Jump)

Atomically, load the **Status**, **PC** (plus **t9**), and **SP** registers. While a **LDST** is used to replace the state of the machine with a new state, **LDCXT** allows a current process to change its operating mode/context: turn on/off interrupt masks, turn on user mode, and at the same time change the location of execution.

This instruction requires the processor to be in kernel-mode, otherwise a Breakpoint exception is raised.

C usage:

```
void LDCXT (unsigned int stackPtr,
          unsigned int status, unsigned int pc)
```
where stackPtr, status, and pc contain the new values for their namesake registers.

7.3.5 INITCPU - (Re)Start a Processor

Initializes a processor to begin execution. At μMPS3 startup/reset, only Processor 0 is automatically initialized. **INITCPU** is used to initialize execution of any of the other processors. [Section 9.5]

This instruction requires the processor to be in kernel-mode, otherwise a Program Trap exception is raised.

C usage:

```
void INITCPU(unsigned int cpuid, state_t *start_state)
```
where

- cpuid is an integer in [0..15] indicating which processor is to be initialized.

- start_state is the physical address of the processor state to be loaded into the newly started processor.

7.3.6 PANIC - Halt Processor: Panic Termination

Displays the text "kernel panic" on terminal 0 and puts the processor into an infinite loop.

This service/instruction requires the processor to be in kernel-mode, otherwise a Breakpoint exception is raised.

C usage:
```
void PANIC()
```

7.3.7 HALT - Halt Processor: Normal Termination

Displays the text "System halted" on terminal 0 and puts the processor into an infinite loop.

This service/instruction requires the processor to be in kernel-mode, otherwise a Breakpoint exception is raised.

C usage:
```
void HALT()
```

7.3.8 New Instruction Implementation Details

Two of the six new instructions (**STST** and **TLBCLR**) are directly implemented in libumps.S. The other four (**LDST, LDCXT, PANIC**, and **HALT**) require BIOS-Excpt handler services. Since entry to the BIOS-Excpt handler only happens when an exception occurs, the **BREAK** instruction is used to trigger an exception.[2] The BIOS-Excpt handler, if **Status.KUc=0**, performs the indicated operation; determined via a code set in **a0** by libumps.S prior to the **BREAK** instruction. If the BIOS-Excpt handler does not recognize the code in **a0** or if **Status.KUc=1**, the handling of the Breakpoint exception is passed along to the kernel in the usual fashion.

Hence, an attempt to perform a **LDST** in user-mode does not cause the more intuitive Reserved Instruction Program Trap exception (**LDST** is NOT a μMPS3 assembler instruction). Instead it is seen as a request for an unrecognized BIOS service/instruction and is passed along to the kernel accordingly.

Technical Point: The BIOS-Excpt handler does not save the state of the processor at the time of a "recognized" **BREAK** exception (i.e. one of the four recog-

---

[2]The assembly code in libumps.S contains the **BREAK** assembly instruction forcing the exception handling mechanism to be activated.

nized services/instructions). With two of these services/instructions (**PANIC** and **HALT**), the BIOS-Excpt handler enters an infinite loop. With **LDST** a new process state is loaded replacing the current context/state. With **LDCXT** the current state is simply modified.

7.4 LDST, LDCXT & the Status Register

Both the **LDST** and **LDCXT** instructions alter the processor's context. This is done either by replacing ALL of the 35 registers that constitute the processor state (**LDST**) or just three of them (**LDCXT**). In either case, the contents of the **PC** (and **t9**), **SP**, and the **Status** registers are always replaced - the context of the execution stream.

As part of the register replacement process, the MIPS assembly instruction **RFE** (Return from Exception) is executed by the BIOS routine. Whenever a **RFE** instruction is executed, a pop operation, as illustrated in Figure 7.1 is performed on the **KU/IE** stacks. This pop operation acts as the compliment to the push operation that was performed when an exception is raised - effectively undoing the shift performed when an exception was first raised, returning the processor to whatever interrupt state and mode was in effect when the exception occurred. Note how the "old" values in the two stacks remain unchanged. [Section 3.1]

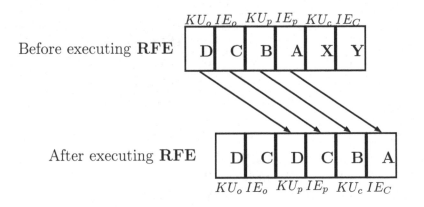

Figure 7.1: **KU/IE** Stack Pop

Technical Point: As when the BIOS-Excpt handler (and BIOS-TLB-Refill handler) saves a processor state, the loading or modifying of a processor state is performed atomically. Since there is no single MIPS assembly instruction to support the atomic loading of a processor state, the BIOS code implementing **LDST** and **LDCXT** loads the new processor state (or modifies the current state) register by register with interrupts disabled. The penultimate step, the loading of the **PC** is performed using the **jr** (Jump Register) MIPS assembly instruction. The **rfe** instruction is executed in the jump's branch-delay slot.

Important Point: When setting up a new processor state to be "launched" via **LDST** (or **LDCXT**), in addition to setting the registers to their desired values (e.g. **PC**, **Status**), care must be taken with the KU and IE values in the **Status** register. Instead of setting the **Status.KUc** and **Status.IEc** bits to their desired values, set the **Status.KUp** and **Status.IEp** values in preparation for the impending **KU/IE** stack pop operation - which will elevate the "previous" values into the "current" bit slots.

7.5 Summary of `libumps` Services

The following two tables in addition to Table 7.1 and Table 7.2 summarize ALL the commands/services provided by `libumps`:

- C-language read access to **CP0** control registers. [Section 7.1]

- C-language write access to writable **CP0** control registers. [Section 7.2]

- C-language access to key user-mode μMPS3 assembly commands.

- C-language access to key kernel-mode μMPS3 assembly commands.

- New commands/services.

7.5.1 User-Mode Instructions

C usage	Instruction Description	MIPS Assembly
int SYSCALL (...)	Request System Service	**SYSCALL**
int CAS (...)	Compare and Swap	**CAS**

Table 7.5: User-Mode Commands/Instructions

7.5.2   Kernel-Mode Instructions

C usage	Instruction Description	MIPS Assembly
void TLBWR()	TLB-Write-Random	**TLBWR**
void TLBWI()	TLB-Write-Index	**TLBWI**
void TLBR()	TLB-Read	**TLBR**
void TLBP()	TLB-Probe	**TLBP**
void TLBCLR()	TLB-Clear	New BIOS service
void WAIT()	Idle processor	**WAIT**
void LDST(...)	Load Processor State	New BIOS service
void STST(...)	Store Processor State	New BIOS service
void LDCXT(...)	Load Processor Context	New BIOS service
void INITCPU(...)	(Re)Start a Processor	New BIOS service
void PANIC()	Halt the CPU	New BIOS service
void HALT()	Halt the CPU	New BIOS service

Table 7.6: Kernel-Mode Commands/Instructions

I think that novels that leave out technology misrepresent life as badly as Victorians misrepresented life by leaving out sex.

Kurt Vonnegut Jr.

8

BIOS Services

8.1 BIOS Overview

The BIOS routines are a collection of functions automatically invoked by the hardware at

- System startup/reset: When μMPS3 is first turned on/reset, a BIOS routine is the first code to be executed: The Bootstrap BIOS routine. This routine sets the stage for the invocation of the kernel's `main()` function.

- TLB-Refill events: A BIOS routine, the BIOS-TLB-Refill handler, is automatically invoked whenever a TLB-Refill event occurs. [Section 3.2.1]

- Exceptions: A BIOS routine, the BIOS-Excpt handler, is automatically invoked whenever an exception (i.e. program traps, device interrupts, Syscalls, TLB-based exceptions) occurs. [Section 3.2.2]

These BIOS routines act as the intermediary between hardware actions and kernel actions. To support this, one frame, the BIOS Data Page, allocated in the middle of **kseg0** (0x0FFF.F000) is set aside as an "unformatted" read/writable frame to hold BIOS defined data structures.

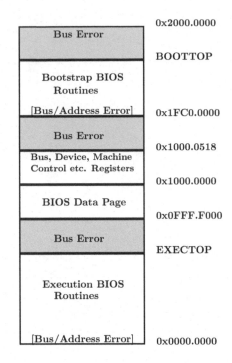

Figure 8.1: Layout of the BIOS Region (**kseg0**)

The following sections are of primary importance to those wishing to fully understand the functioning of the BIOS routines; either for its own sake, or as a prelude to modifying or completing rewriting the BIOS routines.

For projects built on top of the supplied BIOS routines, only a high-level understanding of them is required. Section 8.8 contains a succinct summary of the BIOS services for this purpose.

8.2   System Startup and The Bootstrap Exception Vector

When μMPS3 is started/reset only Processor 0 is enabled. The state of Processor 0 is as follows:

- The **PC** is set to 0x1FC0.0000.

- The **Status** registers is set to 0x1040.0000. This value indicates that coprocessor 0 (for Processor 0) is enabled, the *Bootstrap Exception Vector* bit is on (**Status.BEV**=1), all interrupts are masked, and the processor is in kernel mode.

- All other general purpose and control registers are set to 0.

Hence, the Bootstrap BIOS routine needs to be loaded at 0x1FC0.0000; a process automatically performed by μMPS3.

8.2.1 The Bootstrap Exception Vector

μMPS3 will automatically perform certain actions on exceptions and TLB-Refill events. [Section 3.1] In particular, μMPS3 will load the **PC** with:

- 0x0000.0000 for TLB-Refill events. (i.e. The BIOS-TLB-Refill handler)

- 0x0000.0080 for exceptions. (i.e. The BIOS-Excpt handler)

This is the μMPS3 behavior whenever **Status.BEV**=0.

When **Status.BEV**=1, μMPS3 will load the **PC** with:

- 0x1FC0.0100 for TLB-Refill events.

- 0x1FC0.0180 for exceptions.

Hence, the BIOS code, in addition to defining the Bootstrap BIOS code must also define four routines for exception handling: two for normal execution (**Status.BEV**=0) and two for use during the Bootstrap process (**Status.BEV**=1). It is assumed that **Status.BEV** will be set to zero at the conclusion of the bootstrap process and remain set to zero.

8.3 Functionality of the Supplied BIOS Routines

Upon startup, μMPS3 allows the user to set various execution parameters via the μMPS3 Machine Configuration Panel. These include: RAM size, TLB size, TLB Floor Address, etc. Two other parameters are the location of two files:

- **Bootstrap BIOS**: The name of a file containing assembled MIPS assembly code. The code in this file is loaded by μMPS3 at 0x1FC0.0000. While μMPS3 users can supply their own Bootstrap BIOS code/file, a default Bootstrap BIOS file is supplied with μMPS3:

  coreboot.rom.umps

- **Execution BIOS**: The name of a file containing assembled MIPS assembly code. The code in this file is loaded by μMPS3 at 0x0000.0000. While μMPS3 users can supply their own Execution BIOS code/file, a default Execution BIOS file is supplied with μMPS3:

  exec.rom.umps

8.4   The Default exec.rom.umps

The source code for exec.rom.umps can be found in exec.S[1]
exec.rom.umps defines a number of routines, two of which are:

- The BIOS-TLB-Refill handler: Located at the start of exec.rom.umps so this routine will be loaded at 0x0000.0000. This function stores off the state at the time of the TLB-Refill event and passes control to the kernel. [Section 3.2.1]

- The BIOS-Excpt handler: Located at 0x80 from the start of exec.rom.umps so this routine will be loaded at 0x0000.0080. This function stores off the state at the time of the exception and passes control to the kernel. [Section 3.2.2]

Additionally there are routines in exec.rom.umps to support some of the libumps library calls. The libumps library is a set of routines to support kernel development. [Chapter 7]

8.5   The BIOS Data Page

To support communication between hardware actions and kernel actions, one 4 KB frame, the BIOS Data Page, is set aside to support BIOS defined data struc-

---

[1]The installation process will put both exec.S and exec.rom.umps in the *support* file directory. [Section H.3]

tures. This frame is allocated within **kseg0** at address 0x0FFF.F000. BIOS authors are free to use this frame however they wish. The supplied BIOS code (**exec.rom.umps** and **coreboot.rom.umps**) uses the BIOS Data Page as follows.

When an exception occurs during normal execution, both the BIOS-TLB-Refill handler and BIOS-Excpt handler routines store off the processor state at the time of the exception on the BIOS Data Page at a location accessible to the kernel. One processor state is 35 words long and there can be up to 16 processors/cores. Starting at 0x0FFF.F000 are 16, 35-word areas. The exception processor state for exceptions associated with Processor 0 is found at 0x0FFF.F000. The exception processor state for exceptions associated with processor 1 is found at 0x0FFF.F000 + 0x8C (i.e. 0x8C is the size of a processor state: $16 * 4 = 140 = 0x8C$) The exception processor state for exceptions associated with processor 2 is found at 0x0FFF.F000+ 0x118, etc.

The second action performed by both the BIOS-TLB-Refill handler and BIOS-Excpt handler routines is to pass control to the kernel. Since there are both exceptions and TLB-Refill events there needs to be two addresses for each processor. While **exec.rom.umps** is careful not to use/need a stack, the same cannot be said for the kernel/ Hence in addition to two (**PC**) addresses (for each processor), there also needs to be two **SP** values: one for each handler, which might be the same for both handlers.

The BIOS Data Page in addition to providing space for 16 processor states, also provides space for 16 four-word areas. Each four word area, known as *Pass Up Vector*) is defined as:

Field #	Address	Field Name
3	(base) + 0xc	**SP** for the kernel event handler
2	(base) + 0x8	kernel exception handler address
1	(base) + 0x4	**SP** for the kernel TLB-Refill event handler
0	(base) + 0x0	kernel TLB-Refill event handler address

Table 8.1: Pass Up Vector Layout

The Pass Up Vector for Processor 0 is located at 0x0FFF.F900. The Pass Up Vector Processor 1 is located at 0x0FFF.F900 + 0x10. The Pass Up Vector for Processor 2 is located at 0x0FFF.F900 + 0x20, etc.

Important Point: One of the first tasks the operating system needs to perform at startup is the loading of the Pass Up Vector. Specifically:

- 0x0FFF.F900 with the address of the kernel handler for TLB-Refill events.

- 0x0FFF.F900 + 0x04 with the address of **SP** for the kernel.

- 0x0FFF.F900 + 0x08 with the address of the kernel handler for exceptions.

- 0x0FFF.F900 + 0x0C with the address of **SP** for the kernel.

The starting address for a processor's 35 word exception processor state is "cached" at 0x1000.040C, and the starting address for that processor's Pass Up Vector is "cached" at 0x1000.0410. These addresses are banked (each processor has their own copy). These cached values are used solely by the BIOS routines to avoid repeated address calculations. [Section 9.2.2]

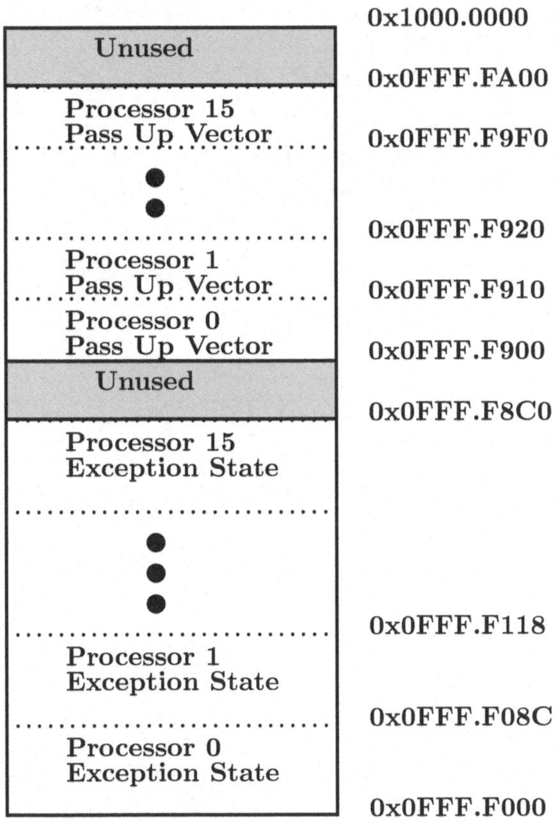

Figure 8.2: Layout of the BIOS Data Page

8.6   The Default **coreboot.rom.umps**

The source code for coreboot.rom.umps can be found in coreboot.S.[2] coreboot.rom.umps defines three routines:

- The Bootstrap BIOS routine.

- The Bootstrap BIOS handler for TLB-Refill events. Located at 0x100 from the start of coreboot.rom.umps so this routine will be loaded at 0x1FC0.0100.

- The Bootstrap BIOS handler for exceptions. Located at 0x180 from the start of coreboot.rom.umps so this routine will be loaded at 0x1FC0.0180.

The latter two routines simply call the **Kernel Panic** routine (defined in exec.rom.umps). **Kernel Panic** writes the words "Kernel Panic" to terminal 0 and enters an infinite loop (i.e. halts execution).

The Bootstrap BIOS routine is the code that is first given control when μMPS3 is started/restarted. The Bootstrap BIOS code supplied in coreboot.rom.umps does the following:

- Loads the Processor 0 Pass Up Vector **PC** fields (0x0FFF.F900 & 0x0FFF.F908) with the address of **Kernel Panic**. This is in case the loaded OS does not correctly assign to this location the address of the appropriate kernel handler.

- Sets **Status.BEV=0**

- Jumps to __start (0x2000.1004)

The supplied coreboot.rom.umps assumes that the kernel will be preloaded into RAM starting at address 0x2000.1000. This option is signaled via the Load Core file check box on the μMPS3 Machine Configuration Panel. [Section 12.2.1]

While unrealistic, preloading RAM with an operating system is a highly useful functionality μMPS3 provides to ease the task of student OS authorship. One can eliminate this by unchecking the Load Core file box and provide a Bootstrap BIOS file that first loads the kernel from a disk or flash device (starting at address 0x2000.1000) before performing the other required Bootstrap BIOS actions.

---

[2]The installation process will put both coreboot.S and coreboot.rom.umps in the *support* file directory. [Section H.3]

8.6.1   crtso.S

C programs typically start with `main()` while assembly programs usually start with `__start`. In order to bridge this gap an additional MIPS assembly file is provided, `ctrso.S` (along with its assembled version `crtso.o`[3]) which defines `__start`. This code, which is given control at the end of the Bootstrap BIOS code, sets **SP** to the end of the first page of RAM (0x2000.1000) and calls `main()`.

If `main()` ever returns, `__start()` concludes/terminates by executing **HALT**.

As described above, **coreboot.rom.umps** and **exec.rom.umps** are BIOS code files specified as user parameters on the μMPS3 Machine Configuration Panel. Since **crtso.o** defines `__start` it is technically part of the kernel. One links **crtso.o** with the compiled object files from one's kernel to create the kernel executable. [Section 10.3]

8.7   Creating or Modifying BIOS Routines

Given the pedagogical nature of μMPS3, the system is distributed with the assembled and source files for both BIOS files, **crtso.o** (and its user program counterpart **crti.o**) and the `libumps` library. Advanced users are invited to modify or replace any (all?) of these components.

One example would be to amend **coreboot.rom.umps** to read in the kernel executable from a disk or flash device instead of relying on the **Load Core** file μMPS3 option.

Since these files directly access both general purpose and control registers, their development must be in μMPS3 (i.e. MIPS) assembler. Section 10.6.3 illustrates how to correctly assemble one's μMPS3 assembly code to be used as a BIOS file.

8.8   Understanding This Chapter

μMPS3 is designed to support a wide variety of student projects, including the modification or complete rewriting of the Bootstrap and/or Execution BIOS routines. Much of this Chapter's detail is necessary for such projects. However, for

---

[3]The source file **crtso.S** can be found in the *support* file directory, while the assembled object file, **crtso.o** is in *library* file directory. [Section H.3]

OS/kernel projects built using the supplied coreboot.rom.umps and exec.rom.umps much of this chapter is overkill.

For users of μMPS3 for which this detail is unnecessary, the following is a summary of the important points:

- The system state when control finally reaches main() is that only Processor 0 is active. Its processor state is kernel-mode with all interrupts masked, its coprocessor 0 is enabled, and **Status.BEV**=0 (which should remain off unless inadvertently turned back on). The **SP** is set to the end of the first page of RAM.

- The execution BIOS routines perform the functions as defined in Chapter 3: store off the processor state at the time of the exception and pass control to a kernel routine. The communication channel between these BIOS routines and the kernel routines is the BIOS Data Page, where the kernel routines can find the stored processor state, and the BIOS routines can find the **PC** and **SP** values for these kernel routines in the Pass Up Vector. Hence, understanding the layout of the BIOS Data Page is important. [Section 8.5]

- One of the first tasks the operating system needs to perform at startup is the initialization of the Processor 0 Pass Up Vector. [Section 8.5]

The question of whether a computer can think is no more interesting than the question of whether a submarine can swim.

Edsger Dijkstra

μMPS3 Multiprocessor Support

Originally by Tomislav Jonjic

μMPS3 can operate as a uniprocessor or as a multiprocessor system, supporting up to 16 identical MIPS R2/3000 RISC (integer-only) processors. Furthermore, each processor possesses its own **CP0** coprocessor. All 16 processors behave identically, as described in this guide.

9.1 Machine Control Registers

Address	Register	Type
0x1000.0514	**Power**	Write Only
0x1000.0510	**HaltCPU**	Write Only
0x1000.050C	**BootSP**	Read/Write
0x1000.0508	**BootPC**	Read/Write
0x1000.0504	**ResetCPU**	Write Only
0x1000.0500	**NCPUs**	Read Only

Table 9.1: Machine Control Register Address Map

Analogous to the device registers used to control peripheral devices [Section 5.1], μMPS3 implements a *Machine Control* register set, shown in Table 9.1. This register set provide the programmer with explicit control over the power states of processors and the machine itself. Specifically:

1. **NCPUs**: stores the number of processors in the system. Each processor is identified by a unique integer [0..15]. Each processor stores its id in its **CP0 PRID** register. The `libumps` library provides a `getPRID()` function for accessing the **PRID CP0** register. [Section 7.1]

2. **ResetCPU**: A power state control register used to start up non-running processor.

3. **HaltCPU**: A power state control register used to halt a running/idle processor.

4. **BootPC & BootSP**: Define a processor's startup state; **PC** and **SP** on reset.

5. **Power**: A power state control register to power off the whole machine.

9.1.1 Processor Power States

At each point in time a μMPS3 processor can be in one of several *power states*, which define whether it is currently executing instructions and its responsiveness to external events (interrupt, reset and halt signals).

μMPS3 defines three power states:

- *Halted*: This state represents the lowest power state. A processor in this state will only respond to a *reset* signal, which transitions the processor into the *Running* state, causing it to start executing instructions.

  A processor transitions into this state when its *halt* signal is asserted, which is triggered by writing its **PRID** into the **HaltCPU** register. The halted processor does not maintain any architecturally visible state (e.g. processor registers) in this power state.

- *Running*: This state represents the normal operating state of the processor. A processor in this state responds to both interrupts and halt/reset signals. A processor transitions into this state as a result of external events.

- *Idle*: A processor in this state operates in reduced-power mode. The processor stops executing instructions when it transitions into this state, but it stays responsive to all external events. A processor transitions into this state by executing the **WAIT** instruction.[1] [Section 7.2.2]

  The processor maintains all architecturally visible state in this power state. This state is also often referred to as *standby*.

Figure 9.1 shows the possible transitions between power states.

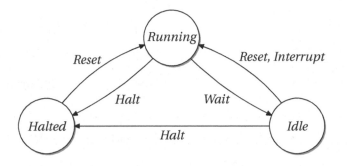

Figure 9.1: Processor Power States

9.1.2   Processor Initialization

After a machine reset, only Processor 0 is automatically started (i.e. in the *Running* power state). Explicit startup (*reset*) commands must be issued to start the other processors. A secondary processor starts executing when it receives a *reset* signal. This is accomplished by writing the processor ID ([0..15]) into the **Reset** register. The processor starts executing at the location specified by the **BootPC** register, with the processor's **SP** register set to the value provided by the **BootSP** register. Furthermore, the **Status** registers is set to 0x1040.0000, while all other general purpose and control registers are set to 0 - a processor startup state. [Section 8.2]

Given the tight interplay between the hardware and the BIOS routines (e.g. exception handling, TLB-Refill events), successful processor initialization must also involve the BIOS services. A libumps function is provided to simplify processor initialization. [Section 9.5]

---

[1]While processor i can *halt* processor j, no other processor can *idle* a given processor. The processor to be idled must itself execute the **WAIT** instruction.

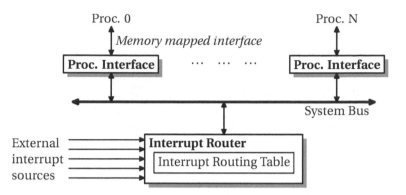

Figure 9.2: Interrupt Delivery Control Subsystem Functional Block Diagram

9.1.3 Powering Off the Machine

Machine power off is initiated by writing the magic value `0xOFF` into the write-only **Power** register. The power down completes after a non-negligible delay.

9.2 Interrupt Delivery Control

The μMPS3 interrupt delivery control subsystem is designed to support SMP-capable operating systems. This subsystem allows for the creation of elaborate interrupt affinity and/or balancing schemes and provides a simple *inter-processor interrupt* (IPI) mechanism.

An invariant of the interrupt delivery control subsystem is that each interrupt is delivered to only one processor. The default settings for the interrupt delivery control subsystem are set to deliver all interrupts to Processor 0 (i.e. uniprocessor behavior).

Conceptually, at the systems level, it is useful to conceive of the interrupt delivery control subsystem as shown in Figure 9.2. This subsystem consist of:

- A centralized programmable unit called the *Interrupt Router* that distributes interrupts from external/peripheral interrupt sources to selected processors.

- One or more *Processor Interface* units that receive interrupts from the Interrupt Router and control the transmission and reception of inter-processor interrupt messages.

The following sections describe the register-level interfaces for the *Interrupt Router* and the *Processor Interfaces*.

9.2.1   Interrupt Router

For systems under heavy I/O load, it is often desirable to distribute interrupts across multiple processors. μMPS3 allows one to specify interrupt routing information per interrupt source. Routing information is stored in a set of programmable registers, the *Interrupt Routing Table* (IRT). Each IRT entry controls interrupt delivery for a single interrupt source.

Two distribution policies are supported:

- *Static:* The interrupt is delivered to a preselected processor.

- *Dynamic:* The interrupt is delivered to the processor executing the lowest priority task.

31	28		15		0
	RP			Destination	

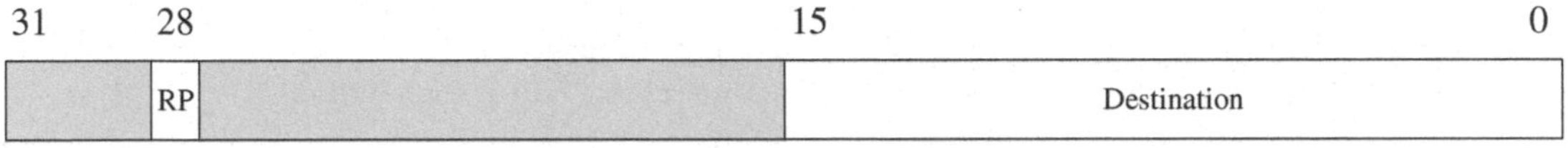

Figure 9.3: IRT Entry Format

Each IRT entry register (Figure 9.3) consists of:

- **RP**: bit 28 - Specifies the routing policy. The field is interpreted as follows:

0 (Static)	The interrupt is delivered to the single processor specified in the **Destination** field.
1 (Dynamic)	The interrupt is delivered to one of the possibly many processors indicated in the **Destination** field. The interrupt is delivered to the processor executing the lowest priority task among all contestants indicated in the **Destination** field. In case of a tie, resolution is achieved via an implementation-defined arbitration mechanism. Dynamic interrupt routing requires the operating system to update at appropriate times the execution priority of the selected processors. This is accomplished by programming the *Task Priority* (**TPR**) register, located in the Processor Interface register bank. [Section 9.2.2]

- **Destination**: bits 0-15 - Used to specify the interrupt target processor(s). This field is interpreted differently depending on the setting of the **RP** bit.

  When **RP=0**, the **Destination** field's lowest four bits are interpreted as a Processor ID ($[0..15]$).

  When **RP=1**, the **Destination** field is interpreted as a processor mask, where bit i of **Destination[15:0]** corresponds to processor ID i.

Figure 9.4 illustrates the complete Interrupt Routing Table with 48 entries. Interrupt routing information for device device j, attached to interrupt line i, is recorded in entry $(i - 2) \times 8 + j$.

Interrupt lines 0 (IPI) & 1 (Processor Local Timer) are never routed via programmer control. Interrupt line 2 (Interval Timer), may be routed, but there is only one instance of the Interval Timer. Each of lines 3–7 may have up to eight instances for each device (interrupt line) class.

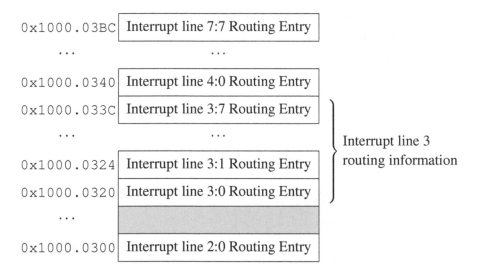

Figure 9.4: Interrupt Routing Table Register Address Map

9.2.2 Processor Interface

The processor interface registers [Table 9.2] represent the per-processor component of the interrupt delivery controller register-level interface. Each processor has its own private instance of the processor interface registers. Each processor accesses its private processor interface at the same addresses shown below.

Though multiple banks (one per processor) of these registers are provided, they all share the same address map.

Address	Register	Type
0x1000.0410	**BIOSReserved2**	Read/Write
0x1000.040C	**BIOSReserved1**	Read/Write
0x1000.0408	**TPR**	Read/Write
0x1000.0404	**Outbox**	Write Only
0x1000.0400	**Inbox**	Read/Write

Table 9.2: Interrupt Delivery Controller Processor Interface Register Map

The **Inbox** and **Outbox** registers are used for inter-processor interrupts; Section 9.4.

The *Task Priority* (**TPR**) register [Figure 9.5] is used by the Interrupt Router for its priority based arbitration scheme. The **TPR.Priority** field allows for 16 priority levels, with 0 and 15 representing the highest and lowest priorities respectively.

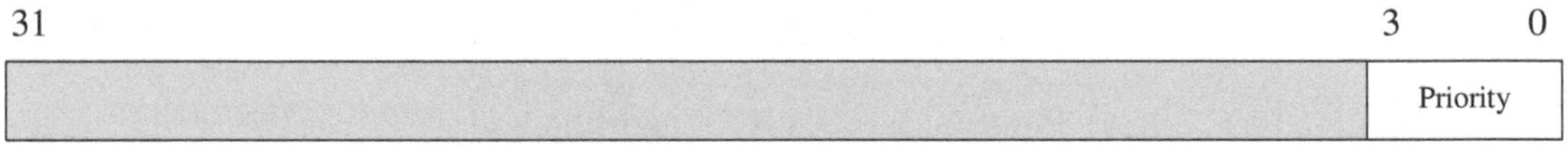

31   3   0

	Priority

Figure 9.5: The **TPR** register

The two registers labelled as *BIOS Reserved* are provided for the convenience of the BIOS exception handling routines. Specifically,

- **BIOSReserved1** caches the address in the BIOS Data Page where this processor's exception processor state is stored. (0x0FFF.F000 + (0x8c * **PRID**)) [Section 8.5]

- **BIOSReserved2** caches the address in the BIOS Data Page where this processor's 4-word Pass Up Vector is located. (0x0FFF.F900 + (0x10 * **PRID**)) [Section 8.5]

9.3 Device Register Memory Map - The Complete Picture

Figures 4.1 (page 24), 5.2 (page 31) and 6.2 (page 45) are, from the multiprocessor perspective, incomplete. Figure 9.6 is a more complete image of the device register area(s), illustrating the relative placement of

- Bus Register Area (Interval Timer, TOD clock, etc.)

- Installed Devices Bitmap and Interrupting Devices Bitmap

- Interrupt lines 3–7 Device Registers

- Interrupt Routing Table

- Processor Interface Registers

- Machine Control Registers

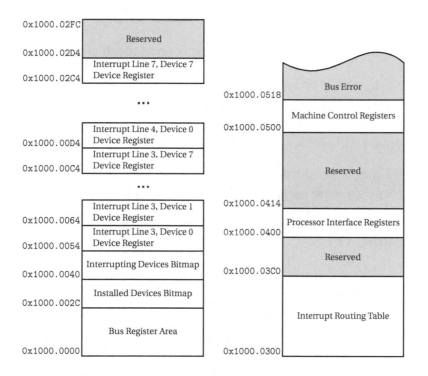

Figure 9.6: Device Register Memory Map

Appendix D contains a complete and detailed diagram of the BIOS portion.

9.4   Inter-Processor Interrupts (IPI's)

An inter-processor interrupt (IPI) represents an inter-processor signaling mechanism used by a processor to request the attention of another processor. IPI's are commonly used by operating systems for issuing rescheduling requests, maintaining TLB consistency, and any other task which requires one processor to request the attention of another.

The characteristics of IPI's in μMPS3 are as following:

- Each IPI can carry an arbitrary 8-bit data field (*message*). This feature is provided solely for software convenience and has no side effects on the IPI delivery subsystem.

- Processor i can signal multiple processors simultaneously, sending each processor the same message.

- Multiple IPI's may be pending at the same time for a given processor.

- Only one pending IPI may be acknowledged at a time.

- There is no built-in delivery status notification mechanism.

- There is a limit of *one pending IPI per originating processor*. For example, if processor i IPI signaled processor j, processor i cannot IPI signal processor j again until *after* processor j has acknowledged the first IPI from processor i. IPI signal requests that violate this limit are ignored.

- μMPS3 maintains IPI delivery order. IPI messages are always retrieved in the order they were received by the processor interface.

9.4.1   Issuing IPI's

Figure 9.7: Outbox Register

An IPI is issued by writing a correctly formatted IPI command to the issuing processor's **Outbox** register. [Figure 9.7]

The fields in the **Outbox** register are defined as follows:

- **Message** (bits 0-7): The message to be delivered.

- **Recipients** (bits 8-23): is interpreted as a processor mask, where bit i of **Recipients[23:8]** corresponds to processor ID $i - 8$. An IPI is signaled to processor i if **Recipients**$[i + 8]$ is on.

9.4.2 IPI Receipt and Acknowledgement

31   11   8 7   0

| | Origin | Message |

Figure 9.8: Inbox Register

IPI interrupts are signaled as an interrupt on line 0. [Chapter 3]

When an IPI is signaled to a given processor, information on the currently pending IPI is stored in the signaled processor's **Inbox** register. [Figure 9.8]

The fields in the **Inbox** register are defined as follows:

- **Message** (bits 0-7): The message to be delivered.

- **Origin** (bits 8-11): The processor ID of the originating processor.

An IPI is acknowledged by writing to the **Inbox** register. The written value is ignored.

9.5 Processor Initialization

The default BIOS routines supplied with μMPS3 are completely reentrant with regard to multiple processors. The reentrancy of the BIOS routines require that each processor have its own location(s) for exception processing. [Chapter 3]

Specifically, each processor needs a

- A distinct location to store the processor state at the time of an exception.

- A distinct location for the **PC** and **SP** pair for passing TLB-Refill event handling along to a kernel routine.

- A distinct location for the **PC** and **SP** pair for passing exception handling along to a kernel routine.

These spaces are preallocated on the BIOS Data Page. Furthermore, the addresses in the BIOS Data Page (processor state area and Pass Up Vector) are cached in **BIOSReserved1** and **BIOSReserved2** respectively. [Section 8.5]

The BIOS function **INITCPU** is provided to hide the complexities of processor startup [Section 9.1.2] and initialization of **BIOSReserved1** and **BIOSReserved2**. As with all the other μMPS3 BIOS services, this service is "invoked" via the `libumps` library.

C usage:

```
    void INITCPU(unsigned int cpuid, state_t *start_state)
where
```

- `cpuid` is an integer in [0..15] indicating which processor is to be initialized.

- `start_state` is the physical address of the processor state to be loaded into the newly started processor.

This function initiates a reset of the processor specified by `cpuid`, causing it to start execution at an execution time BIOS routine. This routine initializes **BIOSReserved1** and **BIOSReserved2** and then loads the the processor state from the supplied `start_state` parameter.

Important Point: It is recommended that the Pass Up Vector in the BIOS Data Page for a given processor (except Processor 0) be populated with their respective values *BEFORE* invoking **INITCPU** for that processor.

Part II
Interacting with μMPS3

You only think I guessed wrong! That's what's so funny! I switched glasses when your back was turned! Ha ha! You fool! You fell victim to one of the classic blunders! The most famous is never get involved in a land war in Asia, but only slightly less well-known is this: never go in against a Sicilian when death is on the line! Ha ha ha ha ha ha ha! Ha ha ha ha ha ha ha! Ha ha ha

Vizzini - from The Princess Bride

10

Compiling for μMPS3

Programming for μMPS3 is facilitated by a complete software development kit (SDK). The SDK contains:

- mipsel-linux-gnu-gcc; a C compiler; the gcc MIPS R2/3000 cross-compiler.[1]

- mipsel-linux-gnu-as; an assembler; the gcc MIPS R2/3000 cross-assembler.

- mipsel-linux-gnu-ld; a linker; the gcc MIPS R2/3000 cross-linker.

- umps3-mkdev; a device creation utility. This utility is used to create μMPS3 disk devices and to create and load files onto μMPS3 flash devices. [Chapter 11]

- umps3-elf2umps; an object file conversion utility. The gcc cross-compiler generates ELF object files. ELF object files must be converted into one of the three object file formats recognized by μMPS3.

- umps3-objdump and mipsel-linux-gnu-objdump; object file analysis utilities. The latter utility analyzes ELF object files while the former one is used to analyze object files that have been processed with the umps3-elf2umps utility.

---

[1]As of this writing, we have successfully tested the series 7 and series 9 versions.

Using the SDK one may produce code for:

- The kernel/OS, e.g. Pandos.[2]

- The two BIOS exception handlers; the Execution BIOS routines (which include the BIOS-Excpt handler and the BIOS-TLB-Refill handler), and the Bootstrap BIOS routines (Bootstrap BIOS). [Section 8.3]

- User programs (U-proc's[3]) that your OS (e.g. Pandos) will run.

Furthermore, one can program either in C or the μMPS3 assembler language, i.e. the MIPS R2/3000 assembler language – integer instruction set only.

10.1   A Word About Endian-ness

Unlike most processor architectures, the MIPS R2/3000 supports both big-endian and little-endian processing - though not simultaneously, the choice is "pin-settable." Similarly, μMPS3 supports both big-endian and little-endian processing; the endian-ness of μMPS3 is whatever the endian-ness of the host machine μMPS3 happens to be running on. (e.g. i386 architectures are little-endian, while Sun Sparcs are big-endian.) As described in Chapter 12, regardless of the endian-ness of the host machine, the trace window's hexadecimal output is always displayed in big-endian format while the window's ASCII output is always displayed in little-endian format.

The μMPS3 SDK tools mipsel-linux-gnu-gcc, mipsel-linux-gnu-as, mipsel-linux-gnu-ld, and mipsel-linux-gnu-objdump are the little-endian versions; for running on little-endian host machines such as i386-based machines. There is an equivalent set of SDK tools for running on big-endian machines. These are named, mips-linux-gnu-gcc, mips-linux-gnu-as, mips-linux-gnu-ld, and mips-linux-gnu-objdump respectively.

---

[2]Pandos is the an accompanying student OS development project. See the Student Guide to the Pandos Project available from the Virtual Square Lab. See virtualsquare.org/umps

[3]U-proc is the term used in the Pandos project to indicate a user program running in the **kuseg** logical address space. This term is used throughout this chapter to represent such differently configured (from the OS) end-user programs.

10.2   C Language Software Development

Programming in C does not easily support module/ADT encapsulation and protection. Appendix G outlines a strategy for implementing encapsulation using C.

Runtime C-library support utilities are –obviously– not available. This includes I/O statements (e.g. `printf` from `stdio.h`), storage allocation calls (e.g. `malloc`) and file manipulation methods. In general any C-library method that interfaces with the operating system is not supported; μMPS3 does not have an OS to support these calls - unless you write one to do so. The `libumps` library is the only support library available. [Chapter 7]

μMPS3 programming requires a number of conventions for program structure and register usage that must be followed. Most of these are automatically enforced by the compiler, nevertheless there are a few that must be explicitly followed.

- The μMPS3 linker requires a small function, named `__start()`. This function is to be the entry point to the program being linked. Typically `__start()` will initialize some registers and then call `main()`. After `main()` concludes, control is returned to `__start()` which should perform some appropriate termination service. Two such functions, written in μMPS3 assembler, are provided:

  - crtso.o This file is to be used when linking together the files for the kernel/OS.[4] The version of `__start()` in this file assumes that the program (i.e. kernel) is loaded in RAM beginning at 0x2000.1000. Various registers are initialized including the stack pointer (**SP**) which is initialized to the end of the first page of RAM (0x2000.1000) - stacks in μMPS3 grow "downward" from high memory to low memory. If `main()` returns, `__start()` concludes by invoking the **HALT** instruction. [Section 8.6.1]

  - crti.o This file is to be used when linking together the files for individual U-proc's.[5] The version of `__start()` in this file assumes that the program's (i.e. U-proc's) header has 0x8000.0000 as its starting logical address. Various registers are initialized but not the stack pointer (**SP**). `__start()` assumes that the kernel will initialize **SP**

---

[4]The source code file crtso.S can be found in the *support* file directory, while the assembled object file, crtso.o is located in the *library* file directory. [Section H.3]

[5]The source code file crti.S can be found in *support* file directory, while the assembled object file, crti.o is located in the *library* file directory. [Section H.3]

(e.g. 0xC000.0000). When `main()` returns, `__start()` loads **a0** with a meaningful value (e.g. 2) and executes the **SYSCALL** instruction.

- The *Global Pointer* register, denoted **$GP**, needs to point into the middle of a data structure called the *Global Offset Table* (GOT). The compiler, by generating (the GOT and) code that uses both the **$GP** and the GOT (located somewhere in a program's *data* section), can improve the efficiency of the linking stage and the execution speed of the resulting code. The **$GP** therefore needs to be recomputed across procedure calls. The general purpose register **t9**, which by convention holds a procedure's starting address, is used for this purpose. While the code to do all this is automatically generated by the compiler, the OS programmer needs to initialize **t9** whenever a processor state's **PC** is set/initialized to a function. Therefore whenever one assigns a value to a processor state's **PC** one must also assign the same value to that state's **t9** (a.k.a. `s_t9`). [Appendix A]

- Given the load/store nature of μMPS3 and the MIPS R2/3000 architecture which it is based on, the code generated by the cross-compiler may bear little resemblance to the original source code. This is especially true if one turns on compiler optimization; which one should NEVER do when programming for μMPS3. Nevertheless, even without optimization enabled, the compiler will endeavor to keep what it perceives to be often used variables in registers.

  This behavior can present problems, especially when the memory location of a variable is part of a device register (or any other hardware dependent location). The compiler may, in this case, move the variable into a register to speed up the code. Any alteration to the original variable (i.e. hardware update of the device register) will be unseen since any subsequent reference to the original variable is replaced by a register reference – which has not been updated.

  To avoid this anomalous behavior all accesses to hardware defined locations should be through pointers since "caching" the pointer's value in a register will not affect behavior. While what the pointer might point at may be updated by the hardware, the pointer's value itself will remain constant.

  In the spirit of it being better to be safe rather than sorry it is probably a good idea to also make liberal use of C's `volatile` modifier/keyword. Any variable declared as `volatile` is never "cached" in a register to improve code performance. It is recommended that all important variables/structures be declared as `volatile`. This would include all kernel data structures, i.e. semaphores, Page Table's, swap/frame pool, etc.

10.3   μMPS3 File Formats

The cross-compiler and cross-linker generate code in the *Executable and Linking Format* (ELF). While the ELF format allows for efficient compilation and execution by an OS it is also quite complex. Using the ELF format would therefore un-necessarily complicate the student OS development process since there are no program loaders or support libraries available until one writes them. Hence μMPS3 uses three different simpler object file formats:

- *.aout*: Based on the predecessor to the ELF format, a.out, this object format is used for the U-proc programs.

- *.core*: A simple variant to the *.aout* format which is used as the object format for the kernel/OS.

- *.rom*: Also a variant of the *.aout* format which is used as the object format for the Bootstrap BIOS and Execution BIOS files. The *.rom* format is for object files and not executable programs. [Section 8.3]

The supplied object file conversion utility, `ump3-elf2umps` performs the necessary conversion of an ELF object file/executable program into its equivalent *.aout*, *.core*, or *.rom* object file/executable program. [Section 10.4]

10.3.1   The *.aout* Format

A program, once compiled and linked is logically split into two *areas* or *sections*. The primary areas are:

- **.text**: This area contains all the compiled code for the executable program. All of the program's functions are placed contiguously one after another in the order the functions are presented to the linker.

- **.data**: This area contains all the global and static variables and data structures. It in turn is logically divided into two sub-sections:

- **.data**: Those global and static variables and data structures that have a defincd (i.e. initialized) value at program start time.

- **.bss**: Those global and static variables and data structures that do NOT have a defined (i.e. initialized) value at program start time.

Local, i.e. automatic, variables are allocated/deallocated on/from the program's stack, while dynamic variables are allocated from the program's *heap*. A heap, like a stack, is an OS allocated segment of a program's (virtual) address space. Unlike stack management, which is dealt with automatically by the code produced by the compiler, heap management is performed by the OS. The compiler can produce stack management code since the number and size of each function's local variables are known at compile time. Since the number and size of dynamic variables cannot be known until run-time, heap management falls to the OS. Heap management can safely be ignored by OS authors who are not supporting dynamic variables. (i.e. There are no `malloc`-type SYSCALLs in Pandos.)

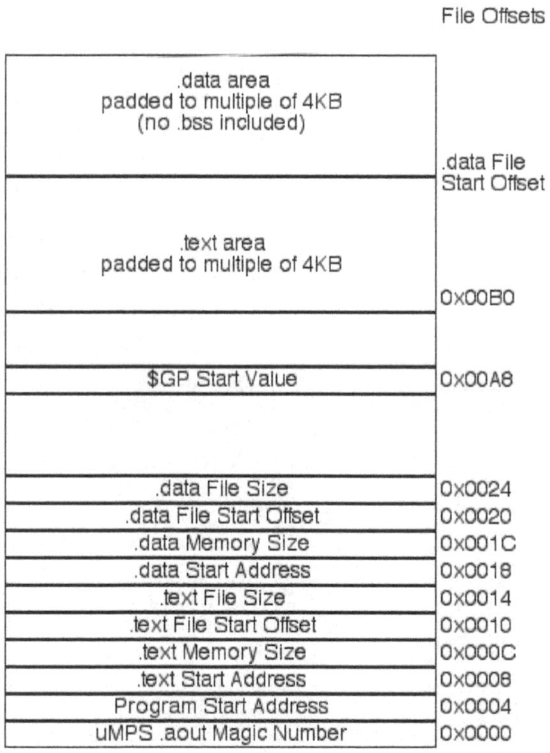

File Offsets

.data area padded to multiple of 4KB (no .bss included)	
	.data File Start Offset
.text area padded to multiple of 4KB	
	0x00B0
$GP Start Value	0x00A8
.data File Size	0x0024
.data File Start Offset	0x0020
.data Memory Size	0x001C
.data Start Address	0x0018
.text File Size	0x0014
.text File Start Offset	0x0010
.text Memory Size	0x000C
.text Start Address	0x0008
Program Start Address	0x0004
uMPS .aout Magic Number	0x0000

Figure 10.1: *.aout* File Format

.aout File Format		
Field Name	File Offset	Explanation
.aout Magic File No.	0x0000	Special identifier used for file type recognition.
Program Start Addr.	0x0004	Logical address from which program execution should begin. Typically this is 0x8000.00B0
.text Start Addr.	0x0008	Logical address for the start of the .text area. It is fixed to 0x8000.0000
.text Memory Size	0x000C	Size of the memory space occupied by the .text section.
.text File Start Offset	0x0010	Offset into .aout file where .text begins. Since the header is part of .text, this is always 0x0000.0000
.text File Size	0x0014	Size of .text area in the .aout file. Larger than .text Mem. Size since its padded to the nearest 4KB block boundary.
.data Start Addr.	0x0018	Address (virtual) for the start of the .data area. The .data area is placed immediately after the .text area at the start of a 4KB block, i.e. .text Start Addr. + .text File Size.
.data Memory Size	0x001C	Size of the memory space occupied by the full .data area, including the .bss area.
.data File Start Offset	0x0020	Offset into the .aout file where .data begins. This should be the same as the .text File Size.
.data File Size	0x0024	Size of .data area in the .aout file. Different from the .data Mem. Size since it doesn't include the .bss area but is padded to the nearest 4KB block boundary.
$GP Start Value	0x00A8	Starting value for $GP, computed during linking. It is usually loaded by __start() into $GP at program start time
.text	0x00B0	The program's .text area
.data	.text File Size	The program's .data area

Table 10.1: .aout File Format Detail

Important Point: The **.data** area is given an address space immediately after the **.text** address space, aligned to the next 4KB block –insuring that **.text** and **.data** areas are completely separated. The **.bss** area immediately follows the **.data** area and is NOT aligned to a separate 4KB block.

.text and **.data** Memory Sizes are provided for sophisticated memory allocation purposes:

- The size of each U-proc's Page Table can be determined dynamically, instead of Pandos's "one size fits all" approach.

- Page Table entries that represent the **.text** area can be marked as read-only, while entries that represent the **.data** area can be marked as writable.

A kernel implemented program loader which reads in the contents of a U-proc's *.aout* file, needs to be aware that the **.text** and **.data** areas are contiguous and have a starting virtual address of 0x8000.0000. The **.bss** area, while not explicitly described in the *.aout* file will occupy the logical address space immediately after the **.data** area. The specification for Pandos does not require zero'ing out the **.bss** area, though doing so will insure that all uninitialized global and static variables and data structures begin with an initial value of zero. Finally, the loader loads the **PC** (and **t9**) with the Program Start Addr.; i.e. the contents of the second word of the U-proc's *.aout* program header (the address found at 0x8000.0004).

.aout (and *.core*) files have padded **.text** and **.data** sections to facilitate file reading/loading. Each section is padded to a multiple of the frame size/disk/flash block size. This allows the kernel/OS to easily load the program and insure that the program's **.text** and **.data** occupy disjoint frame sets.

10.3.2 The *.core* Format

The *.core* file format is used for assembled and linked kernel/OS files.

The *.aout* file format provides enough information for an already-running OS to load and run such a file (i.e. U-proc). The *.core* file format must provide enough information for a Bootstrap BIOS routine to load and run the OS itself.

The *.core* file format is identical to the *.aout* file format with the following exceptions:

- The logical address space begins with the address of the second frame of RAM, 0x2000.1000, instead of the logical address 0x8000.0000. The first frame of RAM is reserved for the **SP**. The **.text** Start Addr. is now 0x2000.1000 and the Program Start Addr. is 0x2000.10B0.

- The **.data** area explicitly contains the zero-filled **.bss** area.

The supplied Bootstrap BIOS file (coreboot.rom.umps) does not load the kernel file into RAM. Instead it relies on the μMPS3 Load Core file feature to preload the kernel *.core* file into RAM starting at address 0x2000.1000. [Section 8.6]

10.3.3   The *.rom* Format

The *.rom* file format is used for assembled BIOS code files. μMPS3 needs two different *.rom* files to be loaded: a Bootstrap BIOS file and an Execution BIOS file. [Chapter 8]

The μMPS3 distribution comes with

- A Bootstrap BIOS file (coreboot.rom.umps)[6] which contains the Bootstrap BIOS routine, the Bootstrap BIOS handler for TLB-Refill events, and the Bootstrap BIOS handler for exceptions.

- An Execution BIOS file (exec.rom.umps)[7] which contains the BIOS-Excpt handler and BIOS-TLB-Refill handler routines.

Given the pedagogical nature of μMPS3, the adventurous student is invited to create their own BIOS files. The μMPS3 Machine Configuration Panel allows users to specify the name and location of the assembled *.rom* files to be used for both the Bootstrap and execution routines. [Chapter 12]

Important Point: Given the need for BIOS routines to directly manipulate μMPS3 registers, BIOS code development must be done using μMPS3 (i.e. MIPS) assembler.

A *.rom* file contains only the **.text** area of its source object file. Furthermore, this **.text** area is stripped of any header information; it is just bare machine code.

The *.rom* format is used when translating an object file into an Execution or Bootstrap BIOS file. The μMPS3 simulator will load these files, place them at their correct addresses and execute their code at the appropriate times. See Chapter 12 for how to load/specify *.rom* file(s).

10.4   The **umps3-elf2umps** Object File Conversion Utility

The command-line umps3-elf2umps utility is used to convert the ELF formatted executable and object files produced by the gcc cross-platform development tools into the

---

[6]The source code for coreboot.rom.umps can be found in coreboot.S. The installation process will put both coreboot.S and coreboot.rom.umps in the *support* file directory. [Section H.3]

[7]The source code for exec.rom.umps can be found in exec.S. The installation process will put both exec.S and exec.rom.umps in the *support* file directory. [Section H.3]

.core, *.rom*, and *.aout* formatted files required by μMPS3.

umps3-elf2umps [-v] [-m] {-k | -b | -a} <**file**>

where

- **file** is the executable or object file to be converted.

- -v: optional Flag to produce verbose output during the conversion process.

- -m: optional flag to generate the .stab symbol table map file associated with **file**.

- -k: Flag to produce a *.core* formatted file. This flag can only be used with an executable file. A *.stab* file is automatically produced with this option.

- -b: Flag to produce a *.rom* formatted file. This flag can only be used with an object file that does not contain relocations.

- -a: Flag to produce a *.aout* formatted file. This flag can only be used with an executable file.

A successful conversion will produce a file by the name of **file.core.umps**, **file.rom.umps**, or **file.aout.umps** accordingly.

A *.stab* file is a text file containing a one-line μMPS3-specific header and the contents of the symbol table from the ELF-formatted input **file**. It is used by the μMPS3 simulator to map **.text** and **.data** locations to their symbolic, i.e. kernel/OS source code, names. Hence the automatic generation of the .stab file whenever a *.core* file is produced. Since .stab files are text files one can also examine/modify them using traditional text-processing tools.

In addition to its utility in tracking down errors in the umps3-elf2umps program (which hopefully no longer exist), the -v flag is of general interest since it illustrates which ELF sections were found and produced and the resulting header data for *.core* and *.aout* files. For *.rom* files, the -v flag also displays the BIOS code size obtained during file conversion.

10.5 The **umps3-objdump** Object File Analysis Utility

The command-line umps3-objdump utility is used to analyze object files created by umps3-elf2umps. This utility performs the same functions as mipsel-linux-gnu-objdump (or mips-linux-gnu-objdump) which is included in the cross-platform development tool set. umps3-objdump is used to analyze *.core*, *.rom*, and *.aout* object files while mipsel-linux-gnu-objdump is used to analyze ELF-formatted object files.

umps3-objdump [-h] [-d] [-x] [-b] [-a] <**file.umps**>

where

- **file.umps** is the *.core*, *.rom*, and *.aout* object file to be analyzed.

- -h: Optional flag to show the *.aout* program header, if present.

- -d: Optional flag to "disassemble" and display the **.text** area in **file.umps**. This is an "assembly" dump of the code, thus it will contain load and branch delay slots; differing from the machine language version of the same code.

- -x: Optional flag to produce a complete little-endian format hexadecimal word dump of **file.umps**. Zero-filled blocks will be skipped and marked with *asterisks*. The output will appear identical regardless of whether **file.umps** is little-endian or big-endian.

- -b: Optional flag to produce a complete byte dump of **file.umps**. Zero-filled blocks will be skipped and marked with *asterisks*. Unlike with the -x flag, the endian-format of the output will depend on the endian-ness of **file.umps**; i.e. if **file.umps** is big-endian than the output will be big-endian.

- -a: flag to perform all of the above optional operations.

The output from umps3-objdump is directed to stdout.

10.6   Putting It All Together: The Development Toolchain

The proceeding sections expand in great detail on the minutiae of code development for μMPS3. This section provides concrete summary examples to help put it all together. The examples assume execution on a little-endian host machine.[8]

10.6.1   Creating an Operating System (*.core*) File

Consider the (unrealistic) case where one's operating system is implemented across three files; partA.c, partB.c, and partC.c.[9]

One should compile the three source files separately using the following compiler flags

---

[8]As documented above (Section 10.1), if one is working on a big-endian machine one should modify the commands appropriately; substitute mips- for mipsel-.

[9]Each of these files most likely also includes libumps.h for access to BIOS services/instructions and **CP0** registers.

```
$(CFLAGS): -ffreestanding -ansi -Wall -c -mips1
    -mabi=32 -mfp32 -mno-gpopt -G 0 -fno-pic -mno-abicalls
```

```
mipsel-linux-gnu-gcc $(CFLAGS) partA.c
mipsel-linux-gnu-gcc $(CFLAGS) partB.c
mipsel-linux-gnu-gcc $(CFLAGS) partC.c
```

The three object files should then be linked together using the command:
```
mipsel-linux-gnu-ld -G 0 -nostdlib -T $(SUPDIR)/umpscore.ldscript
    $(LIBDIR)/crtso.o partA.o partB.o partC.o $(LIBDIR)/libumps.o -o kernel
```

where $(SUPDIR) is the location of the *support* file directory, and $(LIBDIR) is the location of the *library* file directory. [Section H.3]

Note the use of the umpscore.ldscript linker script. Linker scripts inform the linker on the layout of the logical address space of the resulting executable. μMPS3 is distributed with two linker scripts:

- umpscore.ldscript which defines the logical address space for a *.core* file – a kernel executable whose starting address is 0x2000.1000

- umpsaout.ldscript which defines the logical address space for an *.aout* file – a U-proc executable whose starting address is 0x8000.0000

Also included is the crtso.o support file containing `__start()`, and the assembled version of the `libumps` library.

The order of the object files in the link command is important: specifically, the two support files must be in their respective positions.

The linker produces a file in the ELF object file format which needs to be converted to a *.core* (-k option) file prior to its use with μMPS3. This is done with the command:
```
umps3-elf2umps -k kernel
```

which produces the file kernel.core.umps and an accompanying symbol table file, kernel.stab.umps. As described in Chapter 12 these are the default operating system and symbol table filenames.

Appendix E contains a sample Makefile for creating kernel.core.umps along with disk device, a flash device and a single U-proc program.

10.6.2 Creating a U-proc (*.aout*) File

Consider the case where one has a user program that one wishes to run on an already existing μMPS3 operating system (e.g. Pandos); testpgm.c

One should compile the source file using the command:
mipsel-linux-gnu-gcc $(CFLAGS) -c testpgm.c

This test program must be linked.
mipsel-linux-gnu-ld -G 0 -nostdlib -T $(SUPDIR)/umpsaout.ldscript
$(LIBDIR)/crti.o testpgm.o $(LIBDIR)/libumps.o -o testpgm

where $(SUPDIR) is the location of the *support* file directory, and $(LIBDIR) is the location of the *library* file directory. [Section H.3]

Note the use of the umpsaout.ldscript linker script; the eventual target is an *.aout* U-proc file. Also included is the crti.o support file containing the U-proc version for __start(), and the compiled version of the libumps library.

The linker produces a file in the ELF object file format which needs to be converted to a *.aout* (-a option) file prior to its use with μMPS3. This is done with the command:
umps3-elf2umps -a testpgm

which produces the file: testpgm.aout.umps

Finally, this *.aout* file can be (optionally) loaded onto a flash drive with the command:
umps3-mkdev -f testpgm.umps testpgm.aout.umps

which produces the preloaded "flash device" file: testpgm.umps

Appendix E contains a sample Makefile for creating kernel.core.umps along with disk device, a flash device and a single U-proc program preloaded on to the flash device.

10.6.3   Creating a BIOS File

BIOS code development must be done in μMPS3 (i.e. MIPS) assembler. Consider the case where one has a new version of the execution BIOS routines:
testROM.S

One should assemble the source file using the command:
mipsel-linux-gnu-as -KPIC testROM.S

Note the *required* use of the -KPIC option to generate position independent code. (i.e. No relocations)

This produces a file in the ELF object file format which needs to be converted to a *.rom* (-b option) file prior to its use with μMPS3. This is done with the command:
umps3-elf2umps -b testROM

which produces the file: testROM.rom.umps

One would use the same procedure, minus the umps3-elf2umps step to create new versions of crtso.o, crti.o, or the `libumps` library.

It's supposed to be automatic, but actually you have to push this button.

John Brunner

11

Using The umps3-mkdev Device Creation Utility

The log files for holding terminal and printer output are standard text files, and which if not present for any active printer or terminal, will automatically be created by umps3 at startup time. Disk and flash "devices" (i.e. files) must be explicitly created beforehand. One uses the umps3-mkdev device creation utility to create the files that represent these persistent memory devices.

11.1 Creating Disk Devices

Disks in μMPS3 are "direct access" nonvolatile read/write devices. The umps3-mkdev utility allows one to create an **empty** disk only; this way an OS developer may elect any desired disk data organization.

The created "disk" file represents the entire disk contents, even when empty. Hence this file may be very large. It is recommended to create small disks which can be used to represent a little portion of an otherwise very large disk unit.

Disks are created via:

umps3-mkdev -d <**diskfile.mps**> [cyl [head [sect [rpm [seekt [datas]]]]]]

where:

- -d instructs the utility to build a disk file image.

- **diskfile.mps** is the name of the disk file image to be created.

- The following six additional optional parameters allow one to set the drive's geometry:

    - number of cylinders (cyl): from [1..65535], default = 32

    - number of heads/surfaces (head): from [1..255], default = 2

    - number of 4 KB sectors/track (sect): [1..255], default = 8

    - rotations per minute(rpm): [360..10800], default = 3600

    - avg. cyl. to cyl. seek time in microseconds (seekt): [1..10000], default = 100

    - sector data occupancy % (datas): [10%..90%], default = 80%

As with real disks, differing performance statistics result in differing simulated drive performance. e.g. A faster rotation speed results in less latency delay and a smaller sector data occupancy percentage results in shorter read/write times.

The default values for all these parameters are shown when entering the umps3-mkdev alone without any parameters.

Appendix E contains a sample Makefile which illustrates the creation of a disk device.

11.2   Creating Flash Devices

Flash devices in μMPS3 are "random access" nonvolatile read/write devices. A μMPS3 flash device is essentially equivalent to a seek-free one-dimensional disk drive. The umps3-mkdev utility allows one to create both slow flash devices (e.g. USB stick) or fast flash devices (e.g. SSDs). Furthermore, the utility allows one to create both empty flash devices as well as ones preloaded with a specific file.

The created flash device file represents the entire device contents, even when empty. Hence this file may be very large. It is recommended to create small flash devices which can be used to represent a little portion of an otherwise very large device.

Flash devices are created via:

umps3-mkdev -f <**flashfile.mps**> <file> [blocks [wt]

where:

- -f instructs the utility to build a flash file image.

- **flashfile.mps** is the name of the flash device file image to be created.

- Filename to be preloaded onto the device beginning with block 0. If one wishes to create an empty flash device but still specify some of the additional parameters, use /dev/null as the <file> argument.

  To load a flash device with a collection of files, it is recommended to initially create a single .tar file from the collection and then use this single .tar file for this parameter.[1]

- The following two additional optional parameters allow one to set the flash device's properties:

  - Number of blocks (blocks): from [1..0xFFFFFF], default = 512

  - Average write time in microseconds (wt): [1..10000], default = 1000

μMPS3 caps the maximum block size for flash devices at 2^{24}. This translates to a maximum device size of 64 GB.

As with real flash devices, read operations are faster than write operations. The read speed for μMPS3 flash devices is fixed at 75% of the device's write time in microseconds.

The default values for all these parameters are shown when entering the umps3-mkdev alone without any parameters.

---

[1]We recommend the .tar file format due to its simple structure.

Appendix E contains a sample Makefile which illustrates the creation of a flash device preloaded with a user program.

There is a theory which states that if ever anybody discovers exactly what the Universe is for and why it is here, it will instantly disappear and be replaced by something even more bizarre and inexplicable. There is another theory which states that this has already happened.

Douglas Adams

.

12

The umps3 Emulator

The μMPS3 simulator, umps3, emulates all of the μMPS3 system as described in Part I of this guide. umps3 is designed to run on any UNIX-compatible platform, though extensive testing has only occurred using Linux variants.

12.1   The umps3 Simulator

The umps3 simulator loads and executes programs developed for a μMPS3 machine. As detailed in Section 10.3, all μMPS3 specific files have a typical identifying "middle" extension (e.g. .core) and the .umps common final extension. While umps3 acts as a faithful emulator of a μMPS3 machine, it is also a sophisticated testing and debugging environment for μMPS3 programs. As such, the feature-set of umps3 in general and its graphical user interface (GUI) in particular were designed to assist students in the creation of operating systems. The umps3 graphical interface provides one with the tools to exercise complete control over the emulated machine, not only through extensive breakpoint, suspend, and tracing facilities, but also by allowing the user to modify both RAM and control registers during execution.

In the hopeful spirit that the umps3 GUI, like actual well designed GUI's, require no instruction and the observation that students rarely read GUI manuals anyway, the following sections are rather cursory. It is hoped that anyone with familiarity using a modern debugging facility will quickly be comfortable with the umps3 GUI.

12.2 umps3 Invocation and Machine Configurations

The μMPS3 simulator is executed by entering umps3 at a shell prompt or into a program launcher. Depending on the execution environment and installation umps3 may also be available via a desktop shortcut (look in the "educational" section).

A umps3 execution session requires a machine configuration before one can "turn on" the machine. The Welcome screen invites users to either open an existing machine configuration file (a JSON file) or to create a new machine configuration. Opening an existing configuration requires navigating to the machine configuration file's location. If one opts to create a new configuration, one needs to specify the filename and location for the newly created default machine configuration. Conveniently, five of the most recently used machine configurations are also offered as click-able options. One can also clear the display of the five most recently used machine configurations: available option under the **Simulator** menu bar option.

Figure 12.1: umps3 Welcome Screen

At this point one has either opened an existing machine configuration or created a new default machine configuration. Selecting the **Simulator/Edit Configuration** menu bar option allows one to inspect and edit the machine configuration parameters. Toolbar icons are also present for the **New Configuration**, **Open Configuration**, and **Edit Configuration** options.

Figure 12.2: New, Open, Edit Configuration Toolbar Icons, respectively

12.2.1   μMPS3 Machine Configuration Panel

The Machine Configuration Window is a 2-tab window. The options should be familiar after gaining a thorough understanding of Part I of this guide.

Panel 1: General Settings

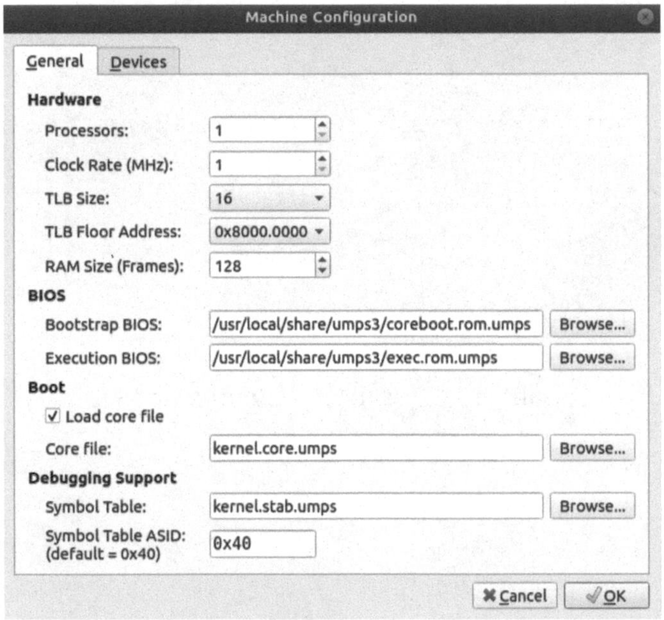

Figure 12.3: General Configuration Parameters

The settable parameters are:

- **Processors**: Default=1, options are from [1..16]. [Chapter 9]

- **Clock Rate**: Sets the Time Scale Bus Register value. Default=1, options are from [1..99]. [Section 4.1]

- **TLB Size**: Number of entries in the TLB. Default=16, options are from [4,8,16,32, 64].[Section 6.3.2]

- **TLB Floor Address**: Address below which address translation is disabled. Default=VM Off, options are from [VM OFF, 0x4000.0000, 0x8000.0000]. [Section 6.3.1]

- **RAM Size**: Number of 4 KB frames of RAM. Default=64, options are from [8..512]. [Section 6.1]

- **Bootstrap BIOS**: Full name of the *.rom* file type containing the assembled Bootstrap BIOS routines. This value is preset to the default/supplied Bootstrap BIOS file; coreboot.rom.umps. Unless one is modifying or substituting the supplied/default Bootstrap BIOS routines, this parameter should not be altered. [Section 8.6]

- **Execution BIOS**: Full name of the *.rom* file type containing the assembled Execution BIOS routines. This value is preset to the default/supplied Execution BIOS file; exec.rom.umps. Unless one is modifying or substituting the supplied/default Execution BIOS routines, this parameter should not be altered. [Section 8.4]

- **Load Core File** checkbox: Controls whether umps3 preloads the *.core* file (i.e. the kernel) into RAM at location 0x2000.1000. Unless one is modifying the Bootstrap BIOS routines to perform the loading step, this parameter should not be altered. Default=checked.

- **Core File**: Full name of the *.core* file type containing the compiled and linked kernel file (i.e. the Operating System). This field is defaulted to kernel.core.umps located in the current directory. [Section 10.3.2] The sample Makefile in Appendix E is set up to create a *.core* file by this name.

- **Symbol Table**: Full name of the symbol table produced by umps3-elf2umps when converting a *.aout* file to a *.core* file. Typically, this file has the same name as the above Core File with a *.stab*.umps extension. This field is defaulted to kernel.stab.umps located in the current directory. [Section 10.4] The sample Makefile in Appendix E is set up to create a *.stab* file by this name.

- **Symbol Table ASID**: While debugging, the symbol table needs an **ASID** value. Since the **ASID** field is only 6 bits, **ASID** values can range from [0..63]. The default setting of 0x40 is recommended for this purpose.

In the majority of cases, the only parameters one might alter are **TLB Floor Address** and **RAM Size**.

Panel 2: Device Settings

The second tab, **Devices** allows one to map various files with various μMPS3 peripheral devices.

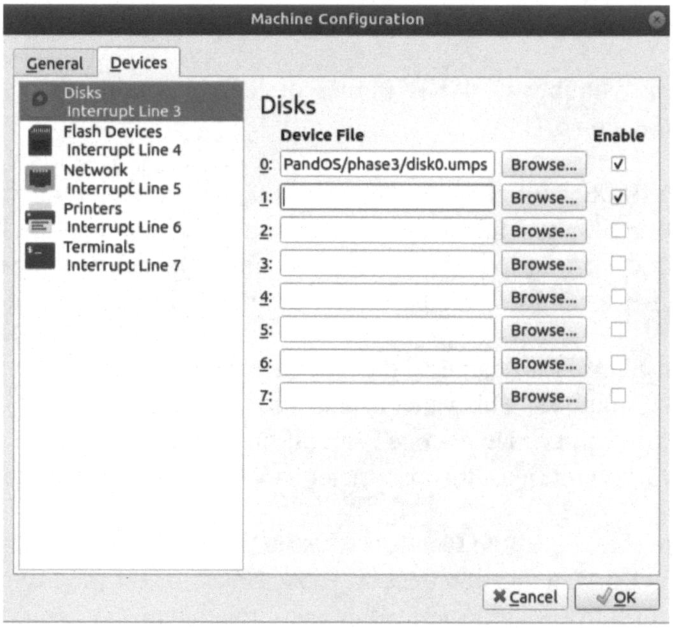

Figure 12.4: Device Configuration Parameters

The files associated with printer and terminal devices are text files which will hold the characters output/transmitted to each device; i.e. a log file. If a printer or terminal's log file does not exist when umps3 starts, its file is automatically created.

The files associated with disk and flash devices are special files created using the umps3-mkdev device creation utility. These files must already exist when umps3 is started. [Chapter 11]

Important Point: Don't forget to check the **Enable** box next to any device you intend to use.

One can always return and edit a machine configuration. One can, however, only edit a machine configuration if the machine is powered down.

12.3   Using umps3

The umps3 "Power Button" is the Green (umps3 currently off)/red (umps3 currently on) bullseye Toolbar icon. The other icons in the Toolbar are:

- Reset: (*Yellow Circular Arrows* icon): Return an already running machine to a just powered-on state. umps3 does not need to be stopped to be reset.

- Run/Continue: (*Green Right Arrow* icon): Continue executing instructions; i.e. the "Run" button. When one clicks on this button it transitions to a Red Stop Sign - which can then be used to halt execution.

- Step (*Green Arrow Moving Down One Step* icon): Single step machine execution.

- Processor slider bar: This slider bar controls the speed of emulation. It does *not* alter the processor speed - a machine configuration parameter.

Figure 12.5: The Processor Control Bar

While using umps3 one can open many different windows. Including the Main Window. There can also be one window per processor (each of which supports up to two subwindows: Register display and TLB display) and one window per terminal device - which can accept user input.

12.3.1   The Main umps3 Window

In addition to the menu bar and Toolbar, the Main Window contains four tabs:

- **Overview** - This non-interactive pane displays the current values for the Machine Configuration.

- **Processors** - A two pane window. The top pane describes the status for each active processor: power state and **PC** value. The bottom pane enumerates all the Breakpoints that are currently set. There are three ways to set a Breakpoint.

    - Option on the Debug menu bar item.

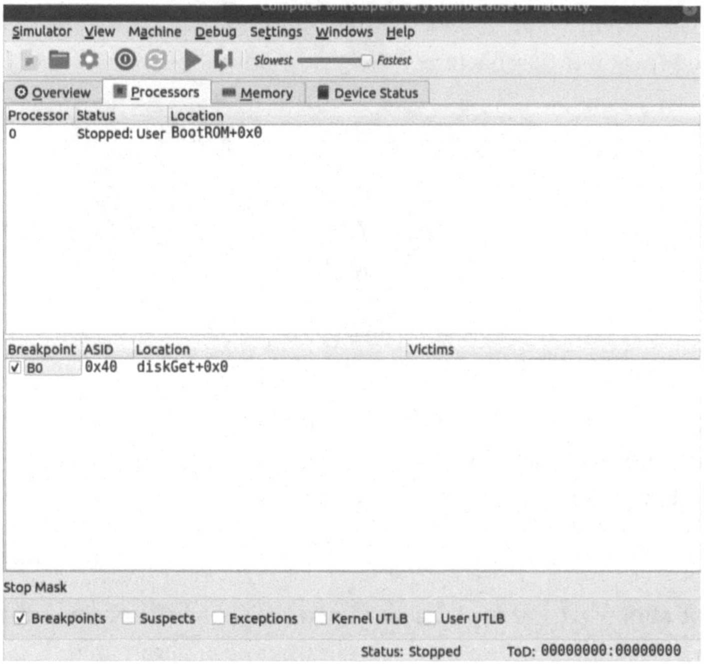

Figure 12.6: The Processors Tab

- Right-click on the bottom pane
- Left-click on an instruction's address in a Processor Window. [Section 12.3.2]

For each Breakpoint set, there are individual checkboxes activating/deactivating this Breakpoint.

When one sets a Breakpoint a pop-up window displaying the contents of the symbol table is presented. Double-clicking (or Single-click + "OK") sets the Breakpoint.

Breakpoints are removed by selecting the Breakpoint and either selecting Remove Breakpoint from the Debug menu bar item, or from the pop-up menu activated by right-clicking in the lower pane.

- **Memory** - A two pane window. The upper portion is for Suspects, while the lower portion is for Traced regions.

  - A Suspect is a memory location (data structure/variable). Execution is stopped whenever the selected memory location is to be read or written. i.e. A Breakpoint for data structures/variables.
  - A Trace region is a memory location (data structure/variable). Setting a trace allows one to inspect (and alter) values in RAM. The displayed values may

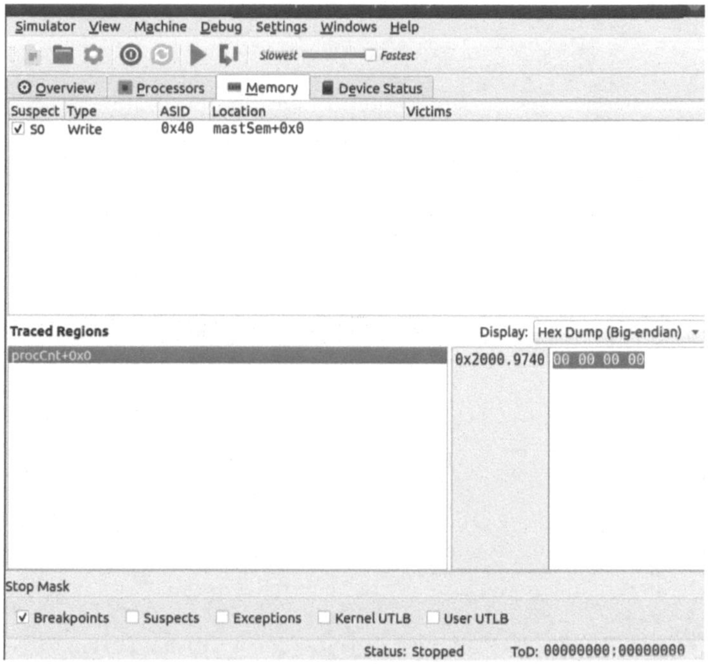

Figure 12.7: The Memory Tab

be shown in a variety of formats. (e.g. ASCII, Big-endian). The default is Big-endian display - even when running on a little-endian host.

Suspects and Trace regions are set and removed in similar fashion: Either via the Debug menu bar option or by Right-Clicks in the Suspect (or Trace region) panes. Removal is isomorphic.

- **Device Status** - Window providing the current operational status of all attached/active peripheral devices.

Breakpoints, Suspect ranges and RAM tracing are the three primary debugging tools. At the bottom of the Main Window is the **Stop Mask**: a set of five check boxes. If a given box is checked then when the appropriate event is triggered (e.g. reach a Breakpoint, write a variable on the suspect list), execution is paused. Hence, setting an active Breakpoint (or other "stop event") is a two part process: the setting of the breakpoint and the enabling of Breakpoints to stop execution via the Breakpoint Stop Mask checkbox. The five umps3 Stop events are:

- **Breakpoints** - when the **PC** equals any of the values for which a Breakpoint as been set.

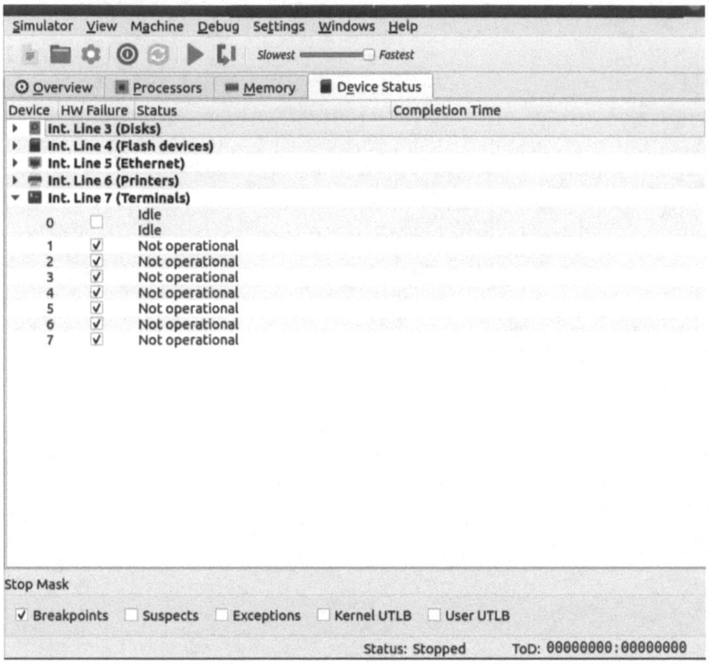

Figure 12.8: The Devices Tab

- **Suspects** - when the target of a load or store operation equals any of the values for which a Suspect has been set.

- **Exceptions** - any of the exceptions as defined in Chapter 3

- **Kernel UTLB** - TLB-Refill events when the processor is in kernel mode (**Status.KUc** = 0)

- **User UTLB** - TLB-Refill events when the processor is in user mode (**Status.KUc** = 1)

The TOD clock is displayed in the lower right corner of the main window.

The Windows menu bar item allows one to display dedicated windows representing any of the (up to) eight terminals and (up to) sixteen processors.

A terminal window displays the text that has been written to it. One also types into a terminal window for terminal input.

12.3.2   A Processor Window

In addition to some repeated menu bar and toolbar items (for convenience), a processor window displays up to three different panes of information:

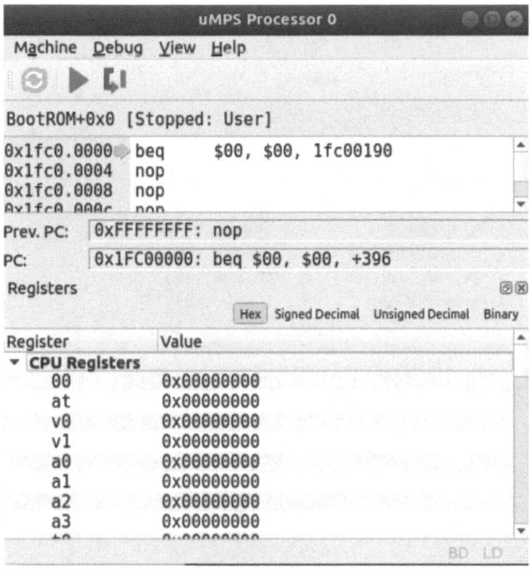

Figure 12.9: The Processor Window

- The Code pane: displays a section of code that the processor is currently executing. While some of the information is updated continuously (PrevPC, PC and function name+offset), the code itself is only updated when the emulator is stopped. Left-clicking on an individual instruction's address sets/removes a breakpoint at that location.

- The Registers pane: displays the 32 General Purpose Registers, the **CP0** control registers and a set of "other registers" which includes the Processor Local Timer (labeled Timer). Given the debugging strategy outlined in Chapter 13 displaying the register pane with the General Purpose Registers **a0, a1, a2**, and **a3** visible will be a common practice. To facilitate the common practice the Registers pane, in addition to most other panes, can be "torn off" into its own separate window.

   Note: All the registers displayed in the Registers pane are also user editable (double click on the register value).

- The TLB pane: displays the contents of the processor's TLB. As with the Registers pane, all the values are also user-editable.

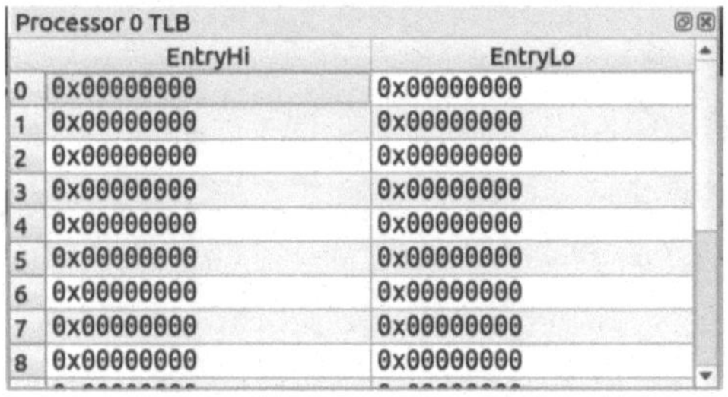

Figure 12.10: The TLB "tear off" Window

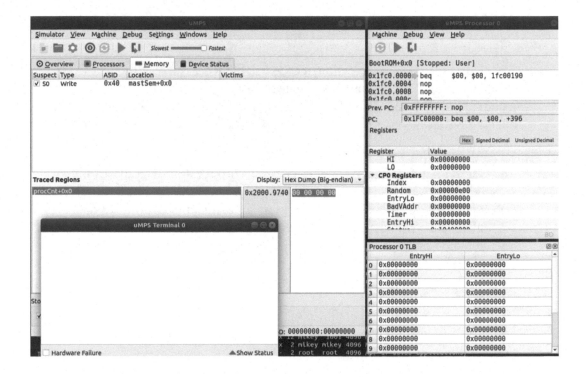

Figure 12.11: A Multi-Window View of a Debugging Session

If debugging is the art of removing bugs, then programming must be the art of inserting them.

Unknown

13

Debugging in μMPS3

As described in Section 10.2 writing code for an OS requires some special considerations. Debugging an OS, unfortunately, is even more challenging. In the authors' experience, most undergraduates, even when supplied with sophisticated debugging tools, primarily rely on output statements (e.g. `cout` or `printf`) for debugging. By examining the generated output stream, students infer both the flow of execution and the program state at each output statement. This can be called "debugging by side-effect." When debugging an OS there is no support for output statements; at least not until the OS author has written and debugged support for them.[1]

Debugging an OS is further complicated by its inherent interconnectedness; frustrating the desire to perform unit testing. One cannot test a scheduler without support for timing services. One cannot test timing services without support for interrupt handling. One cannot test interrupt handling without support for semaphores and a scheduler.

The lack of students' traditional debugging tool, output statements, and the inability to do module testing due to an OS's interconnectedness presents a unique debugging challenge. It is important to start thinking about debugging, not in terms of side effects, but in terms of current program state. Unlike with traditional undergraduate programming projects, where it is possible to test all possible control paths and all meaningful program states, there are too many possible meaningful program states during the execution of an

---

[1] While Phase 1 of the Pandos project comes with its own very rudimentary support for terminal output, in Phase 2, successfully generating any terminal output represents the achievement of a major debugging milestone along the path towards the completion of that phase.

OS for exhaustive testing; at least within the constraints of a term-long undergraduate project. Nevertheless, by debugging with an emphasis on program state, instead of side effect, one can start to gain a degree of confidence regarding the correctness of the OS.

13.1   μMPS3 Debugging Strategies

The μMPS3 simulator, from one perspective, can be thought of as a sophisticated debugging tool/environment. As described in Chapter 12 it provides three primary mechanisms to assist in the debugging process; breakpoints, suspect ranges, and memory tracing. The following is a description of two debugging strategies.

13.1.1   Using a Character Buffer to Mimic `printf`

In the spirit of attempting to force a square peg into a round whole, it is possible to use a RAM buffer to behave like an output stream; allowing the use of the "familiar" debugging technique. To do this one declares a global character array and instead of issuing an output statement, one moves a character string or meaningful value into the buffer. The trace facility is then used to display the buffer's contents. Running one's OS while monitoring the contents of the buffer is isomorphic to running a traditional program and monitoring the output stream.

Writing to the buffer can be done in an accumulative fashion, similar to an output stream, or each line of "output" can overwrite the previous one.[2]

Under μMPS3 one has the option to improve this approach by placing the buffer in the suspect list and enabling the simulator to halt on suspect matches. Now whenever an "output statement" is reached the simulator will stop, allowing for the examination, via the trace window, of the state of OS variables.

13.1.2   Implementing Debugging Functions

The above approach, while useful, has its limitations. There is no `itoa` (integer–to–ascii) function –unless you write your own– so one is limited, via the global buffer, to the display of character strings only. Also while program execution can be halted prior to each output message, only global variables can be examined via the trace window.

An improvement on this approach is to implement either a debug function, or a suite of such functions; e.g. `debugA`, `debugB`, `debugC`, etc. Each of these functions can be defined to accept four integer parameters. Now, at a point of desired program inspection,

---

[2]The test program that accompanies Phase 1 of the Pandos project, in addition to generating output on TERMINAL0 illustrating the test program's progress, also illustrates the buffer technique of writing in an accumulative fashion to a character buffer

instead of generating an output string (e.g. "you are here") one calls a debug function. In this scenario, the first parameter is usually a unique "key" value (e.g. 10, 20, 42, etc) that unambiguously identifies where in the program the function call statement is. The other three parameters can be used to pass along local function variables, global variables, expressions or any other value that will help the debugger understand the program state at that point in the program.

By setting a breakpoint for each debug function (and enabling the simulator to halt on breakpoints), the simulator will stop on entry to each debug function. Furthermore, registers **a0**, **a1**, **a2**, and **a3** will contain the four parameters passed to the debug function. The contents of these registers are always displayed on the μMPS3 simulator's Main Window eliminating the need to use the trace window to display OS state information. Furthermore, unlike the small trace window which always displays all the traced memory ranges, with a debug function one can elect which variables to inspect on a call statement by call statement basis. True, one is limited to only four values, but the trace window is still available to display additional information.

Using a suite of debug functions allows for a greater degree of debugging sophistication. For example `debugA` can be used for scheduling issues, while `debugB` can be used interrupt handling. One doesn't wish to step over n breakpoints related to scheduling while endeavoring to get to a breakpoint related to interrupt handling; just enable the `debugB` breakpoint. A suite of debug functions can also help in the following scenario: one suspects that the Ready Queue is somehow getting corrupted, but only after the first "warm" page fault. Enabling a debug function, say in the scheduler, is inefficient. There will be hundreds of scheduler breakpoints that will occur prior to the one in question. Instead, enable a different debug function in the pager. When that breakpoint occurs, then enable the debug function in the scheduler. Thus one has the ability to enable a breakpoint in a frequently occurring location only after some epoch has occurred, instead of the breakpoint being enabled from OS boot-time.

13.2 Common Pitfalls to Watch Out For

While every OS author seems to generate their own unique errors, and concomitant debugging challenges, a number of errors do seem to reoccur with regularity. The following is a list of some of the more difficult ones to track down. By enumerating them here, it is hoped to save some lucky OS authors from some long and frustrating debugging sessions.

13.2.1 Errors in Syntax

There is not much one can do for a logic error except track it down and fix it. Yet sometimes the logic appears flawless and the code still does not work as expected. This may be due to a syntax error. Some of the structures in an OS can be quite complex; an array of structures, where each structure contains arrays of processor states, each of which in turn contains an array, arrays of PTE's and other data, all of which is accessed through a pointer. While the syntax used to access some value deep in the structure may compile and even run, it can nevertheless be incorrect. It is recommended that by using a debug function to display some appropriate value deep within the structure, one can verify that one's syntax is indeed correct. Even the most experienced of programmers can make a syntax error when mixing together structures, arrays, structures of arrays, arrays of structures, dot notation, and pointer notation.

13.2.2   Errors in Structure Initialization

Errors in initialization are also quite common. Most programmers have grown used to an environment where uninitialized variables are "zeroed" out. This is even true of the μMPS3 cross platform development tools; the **.bss** area for *.core* files is explicitly included in the *.core* file and zeroed out. While the initial values for **.bss** kernel/OS variables and structures is zero, many of these structures get used and re-used over and over. Kernel maintained Process-Blocks are the canonical example. It is important to remember to initialize all of such a structure's fields prior to re-use. Not doing so can make an uninitialized value incorrectly appear to have been initialized.[3]

13.2.3   Overlapping Stack Spaces and Other Program Components

The OS data for one U-proc (i.e. User process) must be kept separate from the OS data for other U-proc's. This is rather easy with respect to each U-proc's virtual address space through the magic of virtual memory. The OS structures that reside in **kseg1** for each U-proc are a different matter. Therefore care must be taken to insure that the OS's data structures for each U-proc (which may include one or more stack areas in addition to a Page Table) are both large enough and completely disjoint. Given the very difficult nature of debugging overlapping stack spaces, it is recommended that this be considered whenever one's OS behaves in an unpredictable and erratic manner.

---

[3]One example of this in the Pandos project is with the support structure pointer field in a *pcb*. A *pcb* that contained a support structure that gets reused by a process without a support structure may appear to incorrectly have a support structure.

13.2.4 Compiler Anomalies

As outlined in Section 10.2 the supplied cross-compiler, even when instructed to behave as conservative as possible, will both reorder one's code and cache frequently used variables. This is especially dangerous when dealing with hardware defined locations –which for compiler-related safety reasons should always be accessed through pointers.

One reasonably consistent, though not surefire way to determine if correct code is being altered into incorrect code by the compiler is through the use of debug functions. Specifically when code runs correctly when "littered" with debug function calls, and runs incorrectly when they are removed, one is probably dealing with the compiler code re-ordering/variable caching problem. As one can imagine it is quite frustrating for a student to belive they have successfully completed phase i of their OS project only to remove all their debug function calls and learn their OS no longer behaves the same.

A (debug) function call is a compiler epoch or bottleneck. A compiler cannot reorder assembler statements that occur after a function call to before it, or visa versa. Also any register-cached variables must be restored to memory prior to the function call. Function calls force a compiler, regardless of the optimization it is performing, to synchronize the generated code with the original source code.

There arc a number of fixes one might try when this occurs:

- Do nothing. The additional debug function calls merely slows down the OS, but does not affect its correctness.

- Try all of the options described in Section 10.2. That is use pointers to access hardware defined locations and use the `volatile` keyword on appropriate variables and structures.

A
C Struct Definitions

μMPS3 is distributed with the file types.h containing the C-language typedef/struct definitions for a processor state, the Bus Register and for device registers. This file can be found in the *include* file directory.[Section H.3]

A.1 Processor State

```
#define STATEREGNUM 31
typedef struct state_t {
    unsigned int s_entryHI;
    unsigned int s_cause;
    unsigned int s_status;
    unsigned int  s_pc;
    int     s_reg[STATEREGNUM];

} state_t, *state_PTR;

#define s_at s_reg[0]        #define s_s1 s_reg[16]
#define s_v0 s_reg[1]        #define s_s2 s_reg[17]
#define s_v1 s_reg[2]        #define s_s3 s_reg[18]
#define s_a0 s_reg[3]        #define s_s4 s_reg[19]
#define s_a1 s_reg[4]        #define s_s5 s_reg[20]
#define s_a2 s_reg[5]        #define s_s6 s_reg[21]
#define s_a3 s_reg[6]        #define s_s7 s_reg[22]
#define s_t0 s_reg[7]        #define s_t8 s_reg[23]
#define s_t1 s_reg[8]        #define s_t9 s_reg[24]
#define s_t2 s_reg[9]        #define s_gp s_reg[25]
#define s_t3 s_reg[10]       #define s_sp s_reg[26]
#define s_t4 s_reg[11]       #define s_fp s_reg[27]
#define s_t5 s_reg[12]       #define s_ra s_reg[28]
#define s_t6 s_reg[13]       #define s_HI s_reg[29]
#define s_t7 s_reg[14]       #define s_LO s_reg[30]
#define s_s0 s_reg[15]
```

A.2   Bus & Device Registers

```
/* Device register type for disks, flash and printers */
typedef struct dtpreg {
    unsigned int status;
    unsigned int command;
    unsigned int data0;
    unsigned int data1;
} dtpreg_t;

/* Device register type for terminals */
typedef struct termreg {
    unsigned int recv_status;
    unsigned int recv_command;
    unsigned int transm_status;
    unsigned int transm_command;
} termreg_t;

typedef union devreg {
    dtpreg_t dtp;
    termreg_t term;
} devreg_t;

/* Bus register area */
typedef struct devregarea {
    unsigned int rambase;
    unsigned int ramsize;
    unsigned int execbase;
    unsigned int execsize;
    unsigned int bootbase;
    unsigned int bootsize;
    unsigned int todhi;
    unsigned int todlo;
    unsigned int intervaltimer;
    unsigned int timescale;
    unsigned int TLBFloorAddr;
    unsigned int inst_dev[5];
    unsigned int interrupt_dev[5];
    devreg_t devreg[5][8];
} devregarea_t;
```

A.3   The Pass Up Vector

```
/* Pass Up Vector */
typedef struct passupvector {
    unsigned int tlb_refill_handler;
    unsigned int tlb_refill_stackPtr;
    unsigned int exception_handler;
    unsigned int exception_stackPtr;
} passupvector_t;
```

B
`libumps` Header File

As described in Chapter 7 μMPS3 is distributed with a library, `libumps`{.S, .o, .h} - source, assembled and header files respectively.

```
/*  External declarations for uMPS library module. */

/* Functions valid in user mode */
/*------------------------------------------------------------*/
extern unsigned int SYSCALL (unsigned int number,
    unsigned int arg1,  unsigned int arg2,
    unsigned int arg3);

extern int CAS (volatile unsigned int *atomic,
    unsigned int oldval,  unsigned int newval);



/* Functions valid in user mode iff CPU 0 bit set in
 *  STATUS register */
/*------------------------------------------------------------*/

/* CP0 register access functions */
extern unsigned int getINDEX (void);
extern unsigned int getRANDOM (void);
```

```
extern unsigned int getENTRYLO (void);
extern unsigned int getBADVADDR (void);
extern unsigned int getENTRYHI (void);
extern unsigned int getSTATUS (void);
extern unsigned int getCAUSE (void);
extern unsigned int getEPC (void);
extern unsigned int getPRID (void);
extern unsigned int getTIMER (void);

/* CP0 register modify functions
 * All functions return the value in register after write */
extern unsigned int setINDEX (unsigned int index);
extern unsigned int setENTRYLO (unsigned int entry);
extern unsigned int setENTRYHI (unsigned int entry);
extern unsigned int setSTATUS (unsigned int entry);
extern unsigned int setCAUSE (unsigned int cause);
extern unsigned int setTIMER (unsigned int timer);

/* TLB read/write functions */
extern void TLBWR (void);
extern void TLBWI (void);
extern void TLBP (void);
extern void TLBR (void);
extern void TLBCLR (void);

/* Idle processor function */
extern void WAIT(void);

/* Store processor state function */
extern unsigned int STST (STATE_PTR statep);


/* Functions valid only in kernel mode */
/*------------------------------------------------------------*/

/* function used to modify the current execution state */
extern void LDCXT (unsigned int stackPtr, unsigned int status,
                unsigned int pc);

/* function to restart an interrupted/blocked process */
```

```
extern unsigned int LDST (STATE_PTR statep);

/* This function stops the system printing a warning message on
 * terminal 0 */
extern void PANIC (void);

/* This function halts the system printing a regular shutdown
 * message on terminal 0 */
extern void HALT (void);

/* Start/reset another processor */
extern void INITCPU (unsigned int cpuid, STATE_PTR start_state,
                     STATE_PTR state_areas);
```

C

System-wide Constants

μMPS3 is distributed with the file const.h containing the definitions of useful system constants. This file can be found in the *include* file directory.[Section H.3]

```
/* Hardware & software constants */
#define PAGESIZE        4096
#define WORDLEN         4


/* timer, timescale, TOD-LO and other bus regs */
#define RAMBASEADDR     0x10000000
#define TODLOADDR       0x1000001C
#define INTERVALTMR     0x10000020
#define TIMESCALEADDR.  0x10000024

/* utility constants */
#define TRUE            1
#define FALSE           0
#define HIDDEN          static
#define EOS             '\0'
#define NULL            ((void *)0xFFFFFFFF)

/* device interrupts */
```

```
#define DISKINT          3
#define FLASHINT         4
#define NETWINT          5
#define PRNTINT          6
#define TERMINT          7

#define DEVINTNUM        5     /* interrupt lines used by devices */
#define DEVPERINT        8     /* devices per interrupt line.     */
#define DEVREGLEN        4     /* device registers per dev        */

#define DEVREGSIZE       16    /* device register size in bytes   */

/* device register field number for non-terminal devices */
#define STATUS           0
#define COMMAND          1
#define DATA0            2
#define DATA1            3

/* device register field number for terminal devices */
#define RECVSTATUS       0
#define RECVCOMMAND      1
#define TRANSTATUS       2
#define TRANCOMMAND      3

/* device common STATUS codes */
#define UNINSTALLED      0
#define READY            1
#define BUSY             3

/* device common COMMAND codes */
#define RESET            0
#define ACK              1

/* Memory related constants */
#define KSEG0            0x00000000
#define KSEG1            0x20000000
#define KSEG2            0x40000000
#define KUSEG            0x80000000
#define RAMSTART         0x20000000
#define BIOSDATAPAGE     0x0FFFF000
```

```c
/* Useful operations */
#define MIN(A,B)          ((A) < (B) ? A : B)
#define MAX(A,B)          ((A) < (B) ? B : A)
#define ALIGNED(A)        (((unsigned)A & 0x3) == 0)

/* Macro to load the Interval Timer */
#define LDIT(T)
    ((* ((cpu_t *) INTERVALTMR)) = (T) * (* ((cpu_t *) TIMESCALEADDR)))

/* Macro to read the TOD clock */
#define STCK(T)
    ((T) = ((* ((cpu_t *) TODLOADDR)) / (* ((cpu_t *) TIMESCALEADDR))))
```

D

The BIOS Memory Region

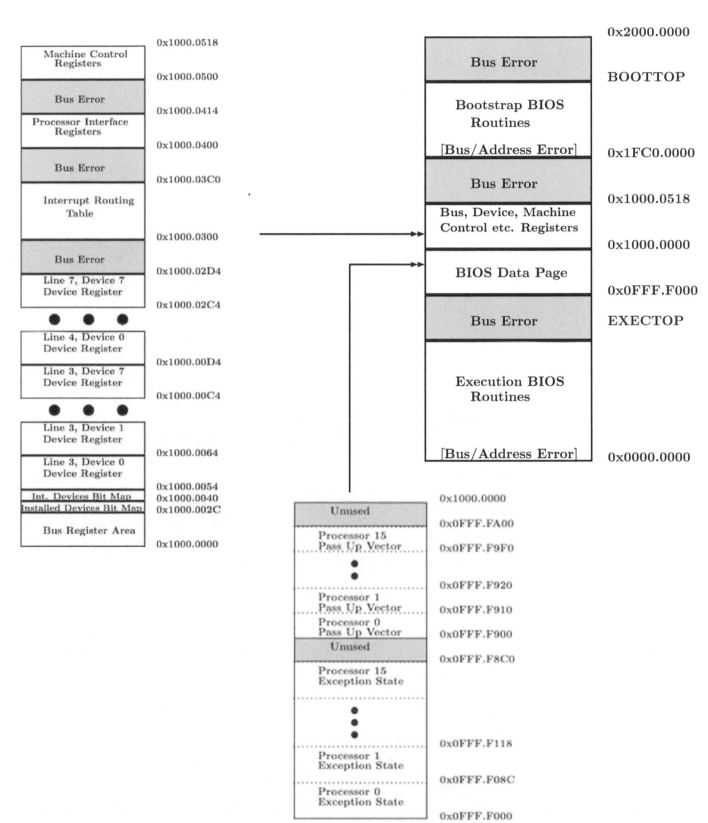

Figure D.1: The BIOS Region: The Complete Picture

E

Sample Makefile

The first Makefile illustrates how to "make" an executable kernel (*.core*) file kernel.core.umps
    The three source files are compiled using the recommended compiler flags. These files are linked together with crtso.o and libumps.o
Note the use of the "core" linker script. Finally, the output from the linker is run through umps3-elf2umps to create a *.core* file (-k option). This Makefile also invokes umps3-mkdev to create the disk0 disk device.
    The second Makefile creates a *.aout* file; a user executable program. The single source file is compiled. This compiled file is then linked with crti.o and libumps.o
Note, the use of the "aout" linker script. The linker output is run through umps3-elf2umps to create a *.aout* file (-a option). Finally, a flash device is created using umps3-mkdev which is preloaded with the newly created *.aout* file.

E.1 Makefile for a kernel.core.umps File

```
# This makefile creates a kernel file from three source files:
ifneq ($(wildcard /usr/bin/umps3),)
    UMPS3_DIR_PREFIX = /usr
    LIBDIR = $(UMPS3_DIR_PREFIX)/lib/x86_64-linux-gnu/umps3
else
    UMPS3_DIR_PREFIX = /usr/local
    LIBDIR = $(UMPS3_DIR_PREFIX)/lib/umps3
endif

INCDIR = $(UMPS3_DIR_PREFIX)/include/umps3/umps
SUPDIR = $(UMPS3_DIR_PREFIX)/share/umps3

DEFS = ../h/const.h ../h/types.h $(INCDIR)/libumps.h Makefile

OBJS = partA.o partB.o partC.o
CFLAGS = -ffreestanding -ansi -Wall -c -mips1 -mabi=32 -mfp32 \
         -mno-gpopt -G 0 -fno-pic -mno-abicalls
LDAOUTFLAGS = -G 0 -nostdlib -T $(SUPDIR)/umpsaout.ldscript
LDCOREFLAGS =  -G 0 -nostdlib -T $(SUPDIR)/umpscore.ldscript

CC = mipsel-linux-gnu-gcc
LD = mipsel-linux-gnu-ld
AS = mipsel-linux-gnu-as -KPIC
EF = umps3-elf2umps
UDEV = umps3-mkdev

#main target
all: kernel.core.umps disk0.umps

# use umps3-mkdev to create the disk0 device
disk0.umps:
    $(UDEV) -d disk0.umps

# create the kernel.core.umps kernel executable file
kernel.core.umps: kernel
    $(EF) -k kernel

kernel: $(OBJS)
    $(LD) $(LDCOREFLAGS) $(LIBDIR)/crtso.o $(OBJS) \
        $(LIBDIR)/libumps.o -o kernel

%.o: %.c $(DEFS)
    $(CC) $(CFLAGS) $<
```

E.2   Makefile for Pre-loaded Flash Device

```
# This makefile creates a flash
# device, preloaded with the compiled test file: testpgm.c
ifneq ($(wildcard /usr/bin/umps3),)
    UMPS3_DIR_PREFIX = /usr
    LIBDIR = $(UMPS3_DIR_PREFIX)/lib/x86_64-linux-gnu/umps3
else
    UMPS3_DIR_PREFIX = /usr/local
    LIBDIR = $(UMPS3_DIR_PREFIX)/lib/umps3
endif

INCDIR = $(UMPS3_DIR_PREFIX)/include/umps3/umps
SUPDIR = $(UMPS3_DIR_PREFIX)/share/umps3

DEFS = $(INCDIR)/libumps.h Makefile
OBJS = testpgm.o

CFLAGS = -ffreestanding -ansi -Wall -c -mips1 -mabi=32 -mfp32 \
         -mno-gpopt -G 0 -fno-pic -mno-abicalls

LDAOUTFLAGS = -G 0 -nostdlib -T $(SUPDIR)/umpsaout.ldscript
LDCOREFLAGS =  -G 0 -nostdlib -T $(SUPDIR)/umpscore.ldscript

CC = mipsel-linux-gnu-gcc
LD = mipsel-linux-gnu-ld
AS = mipsel-linux-gnu-as -KPIC
EF = umps3-elf2umps
UDEV = umps3-mkdev

#main target
all: testpgm.umps

%.o: %.c $(DEFS)
    $(CC) $(CFLAGS) $<

%.t: %.o $(OBJS)
    $(LD) $(LDAOUTFLAGS) $(LIBDIR)/crti.o $< \
        $(LIBDIR)/libumps.o -o $@

%.t.aout.umps: %.t
    $(EF) -a $<

%.umps: %.t.aout.umps
$(UDEV) -f $@ $<
```

F

Compare and Swap: **CAS**

31	26 25	21 20	16 15	11 10	6 5	0
0	rs	rt	rd	0	**cas** (001011_b)	

Assembly Format:

```
casopc rd, rs, rt
```

Description:

The **CAS** instruction performs an atomic read-modify-write operation on synchronizable memory locations. The contents of the word at the memory location specified by the GPR **rs** is compared with General Purpose Register (GPR) **rt**. If the values are equal, the content of GPR **rd** is stored at the memory location specified by **rs** and 1 is written into **rd**. Otherwise, 0 is written into **rd** and no store occurs.

The above read-modify-write sequence is guaranteed to be *atomic* by ensuring that no intervening operation on a conflicting memory location is performed by the memory system. The following pseudocode illustrates the operation of the **cas** instruction:

```
atomic {
    if (MEM[rs] == GPR[rt]) {
        MEM[rs] = GPR[rd];
```

139

```
      GPR[rd] = 1;
   } else {
      GPR[rd] = 0;
   }
 }
```

The set of synchronizable memory locations in μMPS3 coincides with physical RAM locations. For all other locations (e.g. the I/O address space) **cas** will unconditionally fail.
C usage:
```
   int CAS(unsigned int *atomic, unsigned int ov, unsigned int
nv)
```
where nv and ov are integers, and atomic is a pointer to an integer.

This function atomically sets the word pointed to by atomic to nv if the current value of the word is ov. It returns 1 to indicate a successful update and 0 otherwise.

<u>**Technical Point:**</u> The **CAS** instruction is not part of the MIPS R2/3000 ISA, instead it is part of the MIPS32 ISA. **CAS** is one of only two MIPS32 instructions implemented in μMPS3.

G

Encapsulation Strategy for C Programming

It is expected that your operating system will be implemented in C (and not C++ or Java). While C is not an object-oriented language, you are encouraged to divide your code into modules and to try to take advantage, as much as possible, of encapsulation.

You are strongly encouraged to create $i + 1$ subdirectories in your home directory. i of these directories will contain the code (".c" files) for each of the i phases you will implement, and the $i + 1^{st}$ directory, called h, will contain your ".h" (header) files.

The μMPS3 distribution contains two files defining certain hardware-related constants, const.h [Appendix C], and types, types.h [Appendix A]. These will be very useful for you. Copy them into the h subdirectory of your account and make additions (deletions) as needed.

G.0.1 Module Encapsulation in C

You are encouraged to adopt the following set of conventions for programming in C. These conventions were worked out so as to provide programmers working in C some of the benefits of classes and encapsulation.

For an example consider a file (or module) that contains all the functions related to a specific well-defined purpose. This file will contain

- "public" functions: functions that the programmer wishes to be externally visible to users of the module.

- "private" functions: functions that are *helper* functions; ones which the programmer does not wish to be externally visible to users of the module.

- "public" global variables: Variables which are defined outside the scope of any individual function within the file and which the programmer wishes to be externally visible to users of the module.

- "private" global variables: Variables which are defined outside the scope of any individual function within the file and which the programmer does not wish to be externally visible to users of the module.

- "persistent" local variables: Variables which are defined inside a particular function (and hence "private") but, like global variables, have a lifetime equal to that of the program itself (and not just the lifetime, like automatic variables, of the function within which it is defined).

Private components; functions and variables should be declared using the C keyword **static**. A static object, while visible throughout the file it is declared in cannot be accessed from outside the file; effectively creating "private" functions and variables.

A persistent variable is also declared using the keyword **static**. Any variable declared inside a function whose declaration is preceded with the keyword **static**, becomes persistent retaining its value between function calls. Static, or persistent, variables are allocated not on the stack (like automatic variables) but from the same section used for the allocation of global variables.

It is unfortunate that the keyword **static** is overloaded in C. To help differentiate their two uses it is helpful to alias the keyword **static** to *HIDDEN*.

```
#define HIDDEN static
```

Now, private components can be declared as `HIDDEN` while persistent components can be declared as `static`.

For each file/module there should also be an external declarations header (".h") file. This file should contain the prototypes for each public function and global variable. Each prototype should be preceded by the keyword **extern**. Like a C++ ".h" file, any other module that makes use of one module's public functions or variables will `#include` that module's corresponding ".h" file. For example:

```
#include ``../h/asl.h''
```

Finally, global structures (i.e. `typedef`'s) and constants should be defined in appropriate ".h" files; e.g. const.h and types.h

H

Installing umps3 and the Development Tools

The following are directions for installing the gnu MIPS cross compiler and the umps3 system on a little-endian (e.g. x86-based processors) Debian-based Linux distro (e.g. Ubuntu). While it is infeasible to test every Linux distro on all available architectures, it is believed that the following should work for most (all?) Debian-based Linux distros - both big-endian and little-endian. Furthermore, there is nothing inherent with the cross compiler tools nor umps3 preventing a successful installation on a different Linux distro base (e.g. OpenSUSE).

H.1   Installation of the Gnu Cross Compiler and Dependent Libraries

It is always a good practice to run the following before undertaking any package installation procedure.

- sudo apt-get update

- sudo apt-get install build-essential

umps3 is dependent on the following libraries:

- QT 5.5 +

- libelf

- boost 1.34+

- libsigc++ 2.0

- cmake

To install the gnu MIPS cross compiler, associated tools, and dependent libraries:

```
sudo apt install git build-essential cmake qtbase5-dev libelf-dev libboost-dev libsigc++-2.0-dev gcc-mipsel-linux-gnu
```

H.2 Installation of umps3

There are two ways to install umps3:

- Building from source

- Installation via a package manager

H.2.1 Building from Source

Perform the following steps to install umps3:

- Download the umps3 archive file from the Virtual Square git repository and unpack it in a local directory.

- "cd" to the root of the source tree/downloaded archive.

- mkdir build

- cd build

- cmake ..

- make

- sudo make install

H.2.2 Installation via a Package Manager

Given the wide variation in Linux distro package managers and their associated software repositories, we provide instruction for installing on Ubuntu and refer users of other distros to the Virtual Square home page `virtualsquare.org/umps`

For Ubuntu, perform the following steps to enable Universe, add the Virtual Square ppa and perform the installation:

- sudo add-apt-repository universe

- sudo apt update

- sudo add-apt-repository ppa:virtualsquare/umps

- sudo apt update

- sudo apt install umps3

H.3 Installation Directories

In the Unix world there is a fundamental difference between packages installed from source and those installed via a package manager with regard to the installation location of supporting files (include files, libraries, etc).

Packages installed from source install their supporting files in /usr/local while package managers install their supporting files in /usr

umps3 installs accompanying files into three different directories:

- A *support* directory: libumps.S, exec.S, coreboot.S, crtso.S, crti.S, coreboot.rom.umps, exec.rom.umps, umpscore.ldscript, and umpsaout.ldscript

- An *include* directory: libumps.h, const.h, types.h, plus some other .h files of potential interest to advanced users.

- A *library* directory: libumps.o, crtso.o, and crti.o

The *support* directory is either /usr/local/share/umps3, or /usr/share/umps3

The *include* directory is either /usr/local/include/umps3/umps, or /usr/include/umps3/umps

The *library* directory is either /usr/local/lib/umps3 or some more architecture dependent location (e.g. /usr/lib/x86_64-linux-gnu/umps3)

The provided sample Makefiles are built to work with either type of installation. [Appendix E]

I

Format of Key **CP0** Registers

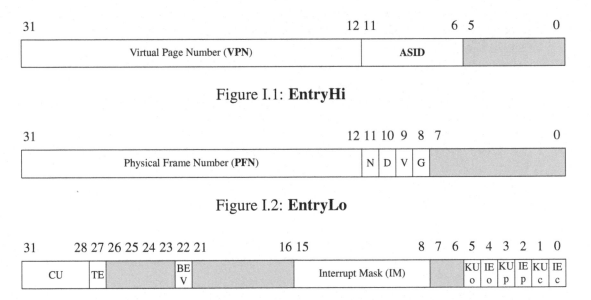

31   12 11   6 5   0

| Virtual Page Number (**VPN**) | ASID | |

Figure I.1: **EntryHi**

31   12 11 10 9 8 7   0

| Physical Frame Number (**PFN**) | N | D | V | G | |

Figure I.2: **EntryLo**

31   28 27 26 25 24 23 22 21   16 15   8 7 6 5 4 3 2 1 0

| CU | TE | | BEV | | Interrupt Mask (IM) | | KUo | IEo | KUp | IEp | KUc | IEc |

Figure I.3: Status Register

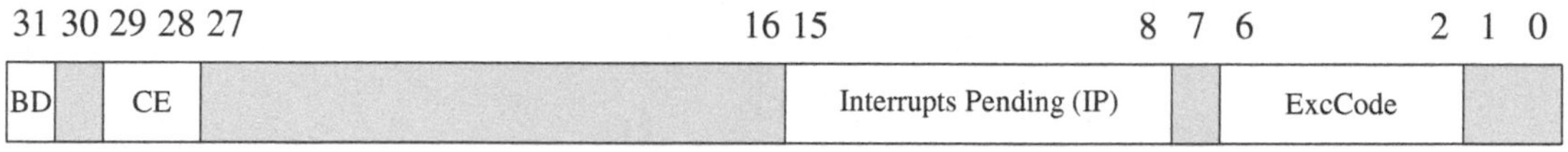

31 30 29 28 27		16 15	8 7 6	2 1 0
BD	CE		Interrupts Pending (IP)	ExcCode

Figure I.4: **Cause CP0** Register

Number	Code	Description
0	*Int*	External Device Interrupt
1	*Mod*	TLB-Modification Exception
2	*TLBL*	TLB Invalid Exception: on a Load instr. or instruction fetch
3	*TLBS*	TLB Invalid Exception: on a Store instr.
4	*AdEL*	Address Error Exception: on a Load or instruction fetch
5	*AdES*	Address Error Exception: on a Store instr.
6	*IBE*	Bus Error Exception: on an instruction fetch
7	*DBE*	Bus Error Exception: on a Load/Store data access
8	*Sys*	Syscall Exception
9	*Bp*	Breakpoint Exception
10	*RI*	Reserved Instruction Exception
11	*CpU*	Coprocessor Unusable Exception
12	*OV*	Arithmetic Overflow Exception

Table I.1: Cause Register Status Codes